The Words Don't Fit In My Mouth
by
jessica Care moore

Published by Moore Black Press
P.O. Box 394 Flatbush Avenue Box 701
Brooklyn, New York 11201
718-826-4135

Text copyright 1997 Jessica Care Moore

Editor: Tony Medina
Book Layout Design: Tyren Allen and Nexus
Cover Art: Pierre M. Bonnett "Brown"
MBP Logo: Aaquil

ISBN Trade 0-9658308-0-2

To: Miss JAlili
Thank you for the Support !!
For I Grew ...
_97_

The Words Don't Fit In My Mouth
by

jessica Care moore

Meditations by
Tony Medina,
Dante Beze (Mos Def), &
T. Tara Turk

MOORE BLACK PRESS
New York • Detroit • London

THE WORDS DON'T FIT IN MY MOUTH
INGREDIENTS:

Asante Sana!

There are many people I need to thank, too many to fit on this page. This experience has been and is still incredible and often times overwhelming. As a "young" writer, I feel very blessed to be able to share my work with the masses of people who continue to support me. To my creator, I had a plan and you had a plan. you won. To my mother, Irene, thank you for the support no matter who or what; and my big brothers, Mark, Jonny, Billy, William and Ed for making me proud to be a "little" sister. Thanks to my sisters, Lisa and Pat, and all the beautiful Moore women. To my Detroit homegirls, Charlotte (What up chuck?) Chamere, Treavion,(yea, yea, you're my publicist), Leslie and the entire Phillips family, Hilary, Jordan and Dresdan, (Mamur!!) Lynn, (never say goodbye), Tureka (my sanity), Nikki, Nicole, Tiffany, my cousins Angela and Alexis, and everyone I didn't name. . . power divas, warriors on many frontlines, but always in my corner. When I read my first poem in "public," entitled "Breeze, " I was in front of an audience of family and friends at my father's funeral in 1994. It changed my life. My dreams of being a writer, an accomplished journalist began to struggle with a new creative voice in my poetry. That's why when I asked Pierre to do the artwork for my cover, I knew the one element that had to be a part of the piece was my father. (He's sitting on the bench sportin' a white suit, Alabama flava). Watching over me.

To Maurice Malone, all of Detroit's underground who keep Motown alive without the convenience of the "rah-rah," to the Pourme Cafe staff: Toya, Tree and crew. Zana and Corey for first believing in "grace." Billy T, Mojo, the Metro Times, Darrell Dawsey, Truth Bookstore,Slum Village, Hassan, Detroit's Muslim community, Cricket, Dope-A-Delic, J.P. The HypeMan, Gary, Felipe, Mark, Larry, Shawn, (where's my moon?) A crew called Open Mic, Khary, Rick, Saeed and family, Guerilla TV, Jess Kickin' It Staff, Shawn P, Jack, Lena, Gena, the entire EmRoup crew for keeping poetry alive; the entire staff at Cody High School, John Perry, Susan Storey, Les Troupe Des Arts, Aurora Harris and all the poetic sistas of Seeds.

To my posse from back in the day, Chip, Peanut, Taco, Mike and everyone else who inspired my life through incredible experiences. The Hawk Family, The Lightfoot Family, The Taylor Family The James Family, and the Dorsey Family. The '89 crew at MSU. Chris Webber, let's do pizza, Jason and Eric, Sedricka and family.

My first two years in Brooklyn feel like a lifetime. I've been touched by so many poets, writers, ordinary people, thinkers, activists, comedians, musicians, supporters, and please know that you are appreciated and I feel honored to know you. To Harlem, your spirit took mine over and I am a child of all

iii

your history. To say that I became a part of that in my own way on the Apollo Stage continues to humble me. To the little sistas who wrote down the Black Statue of Liberty or Black Girl Juice from TV and recited them in pageants or to friends, those poems are yours. Now, write, write, write! To all the brothas who wrote me from prison, know that we are fighting for you and I love all the poems. Thank you. My journalism family at the Daily Challenge, My television family at UPN in Detroit. This book was put together during one of my most rewarding and stressful times in NYC. I've learned the meaning of friendship, love, lost, death, success, failure, fear, beauty, commitment, ugly, pain, joy, happiness, unconditional everything. To my boys who held me together when I ran out of strength, 452, you know who you are. My partna, Josh (Fa-Fa), you saved me in more ways then you can imagine. Tyren-we finally did it baby, Yes Yes. Brad, my voice of reason and one of the most talented artists I know who will eat your food like he actually y made a purchase. Marco, the world traveler. Sharrif, who are you? My brotha, my friend, your cousin? My road dog, no doubt. A stranger among friends. Pierre "Brown" The first man to put calm in my hands even when he was shaking. My soulmate, my friend, thank you for forcing me to read my own work, one breath at a time. We've known one another in many lifetimes. . . Our work is just beginning. To the entire Bonnett family, especially two exceptionally strong women, Pamela and Louise. To my Paris girl, Oui! Oui! Danielle. Mike and the Brooklyn Moon Cafe, Sunday Tea Party, Shield Newspaper, Amsterdam News, Herb Boyd, The City Sun, Afrikan Poetry Theater, Alvin Seme, Ozone Entertainment, all the fly poets on Eargasms, Antonio Hart and Impulse Records. D.L. Hartley, Talib Kwali of Reflection Eternal, Cango from UTFO, Sammantha, DJ Cocoa Chanelle, Native Sun, Mike Ladd, Altered Egos, Black Lotus, The Cold Crush Brothers, Pee Wee Dance, Asante, Dre and Warren. Eddie, Rodney. Weldon Irvine,Nine, Smooth Da Hussler, GZA, Killa Priest (what's up with our song?), Sunz of Man, Razor, Tip, JayDee (where's my music?), Kris Parker for all the support, Ed Lover and Dr. Dre, Kirt Flirt, Angie Martinez, and the Hot 97 crew for everything, Charlie, 4Kast, WBAI, Gary Byrd, WBLS, WHCR, WLIB, Kiss FM, Fatim, Brother Shine for keeping poetry on the radio. Khary-for playing my song in the "D." Vy Higgensen, Ken Wydro and the entire 1996 cast of Born to Sing Mama 3, CeCe Winans (homegirl), Whitney Houston for the kind words, Kevin, DonJuan Holder, Reggie Powe and HeritageCollection, Digital Mafia, Virtual Melanin. My teammates on the 1996 Nuyorican Poetry Slam Team, Saul Williams, Mums the Schemer, and Beau Sia. The spiritual battle is never over. Asha, Kymbali, Tish, Carmen, Leeza, Shakey, Latasha, Serenity, Nzinga, Shawn, Malika B, Fabian, Rhamelle, Kap, Second 2 Last Poets, Jahni, T'kalla, Alexis,Patrick, Jazz Poets

Society, Wood, Vibe Khamelions, Miss Lesane, Lucky, student activists around the country that continue to give me support. To the baddest drummer on the planet, Stix Bones, Pop, Scratch and the Brown family, especially Devita. To some of my spiritual inspiration: Yale (Njoma), keeping me focused, Ken Jones, dropping black diamonds in my palms. Vic, my dance partner always. Khary, is the band all here? Mujahid, for temporary agapa, SteveHaynes, I'm sending you ten percent for all the inspiration. . .you know what's up sabotage. Crazy love. Dante Beze, some NY men do slow dance. Danny Toon, love you blue butterfly. Pharoah, my king, you are an incredible talent. Will "send me an angel" Townsend. My spiritual elders, Abiodún Oyewole and Umar Bin Hassan, thank you for trusting my words, and keeping yours. To my big sisters, others mothers, Estina Baker and Akanke. . .sister griots. Phllyis Yvonne Stickney, for being you. Allison Williams, for the support. The Motown Sound, for all the musical inspiration. Minister Conrad and Michelle Muhammed, Eric Muhammed, and Khalid Muhammed for all the support. Walter Bowe and Dr. John Henrik Clarke for blessing me with your presence at my play. To Ai, Nikki Giovanni, Sonia Sanchez, Larry Neal, Ntozake Shange, Nikky Finney, Jill Nelson and the black literary talent on the planet and off. Gil-Scott Herron, It was an honor to share the stage. Kwame Toure, for making me prove I was a real poet. Tony Medina, for your honesty, input, time and jokes. Black Classic Press Digital Printing, Cheryl Waters, Greg Pulvar for having my back, Faith Childs Literary Agency, the entire Apollo staff, Chuck Sutton, Steve Harvey, Kiki, Keith, Ben and a special thanks to Maurice Dwyer for suggesting I take my poem to the Apollo audience. Maxine Lewis for believing in my work. Grandma Funk, Maria Davis and Rudy for putting me on my first NY stage, Carolines Comedy Club, Donelle Rawlings, Lou Migel, Khahil, Talent, Mike Bonner, Wil, Dave Chapelle, and anybody trying to make people laugh. To everyone I didn't mention. I tried, you are in my thoughts and prayers. To all the hard brothas I made smile. This is a great blessing. I'm still gettin' my lesson daddy. Enjoy.

A very special thanks to everyone who said I couldn't do it.

Moore Black Press

This book is dedicated to the loud laughing, always dancing, down south talking, stubborn, head-strong, truck driving spirit of my daddy Thomas Davis "T.D." Moore of Detroit-Alabama. You always told me to get "my lesson," when you were my greatest teacher. Also to my soft spoken (yea right), big hearted, English tea drinking, worry like crazy, understanding mum, Irene Patricia Moore.

To all my friends and family everywhere.

And to Pierre, who I trusted with the image of my father watching over me in the park. It was one of the greatest gifts I've ever received, during a time when people have given up on giving. Thank you for the unconditional love, the friendship, the calm, and the inspiration.

Four Words

Meditations On Moore

One

No matter the chatter of rogues dressed in high priest gear, constantly wasting air space and paper whining about how poetry should be divorced from politics (from reality), any poet worth their weight in syllables and words uses poetry for certain reasons, be it to define yourself, to defend yourself, or to describe your environment with accuracy, communicating a clear understanding of what is going on in the world.

Jessica Care Moore is a poet who recognizes this. Unlike your usual lot of dry poets shitted out of the bowels of Ivy League Schools and other stamp-of-approval institutions designed to stamp out creativity and promote accommodationist mediocrity, Moore wastes no time beating around the bush about where she stands politically, spiritually or emotionally. In this, her first book, she pulls no punches and takes no prisoners. We are immediately dragged kicking and screaming into her world, her reality, to be pimp smacked awake into consciousness, into her furious fire of hot righteous words, rupturing out of her mouth and onto the page—rage made beautiful by the sheer lyricism simple honesty brings.

In short,The Words Don't Fit in My Mouth is a thematically, multivarious complex collage full of poems on love and lost, relationships, racism, sexism and identity that says: "...we exist/Yes we do? It's a fact."

The poems collected here are kaleidoscopic landscapes seen through drive-by blue bottle stain glass lenses; what her senses pick up from the world around her like bread dough soppin up some gravy.

There is a haunting, painful tone in her work. A defiant, lush, electric lyricism (rough and hewn as Whitman's yawp or Ginsberg's howl) that drives from line to line, image to image, juxtaposition to endless juxtaposition of metaphor. It is themselves the metaphors which she reels out like Hemingway's old man from the sea of poetry, painting word landscapes of black womanchild pain, staring pouty-mouthed defiance (like Ntozake's colored girl on the cover of her first book!) at a world bent on breaking and undermining black women with its indifferent erasure. This is the poetry that Jessica writes, full of tomboy muscle and tender sister love caresses. She coos and curses and condemns—all in one breath, all in one poem, one book.

Moore opts to write socially responsible poetry that speaks for and to a generation that did not benefit from the reforms gained by the Civil Rights Movement. Mixing the somber with the tender and the tender with the straight out bombastic, Moore displays a range that spans poems that not only attack and condemn but cries, comforts, kisses and praises. And she does this by employing quick-flash poetic devices (what I like to call machine gun poetry), possibly stemming from the reality of hip-hop culture.

In poems like "My caged bird don't sing" end rhymes and internal rhyme schemes add to the driving lyrical force of the poem, moving them along quickly.

She could care less about being the kind of poet who in neatly polished poem after neatly polished poem is constantly perpetrating a fraud on reality; she is not down with these emotional liars ignoring the truth about our situation here under the callused, gangrenous heel of monopoly capitalism. In The Words Don't Fit in My Mouth, Moore wants to be perfectly clear.

> People ask why it matters where my people been
> My life is summed up in a break beat
> A semi-sweet half chocolate existence
> Melting in my mouth so I think through hopeful hands
> Aspire to change the rhythm of any land

In "Rising of the Sun," she sings:
> "Poetry be my angel wings
> So I get the holy ghost
> From all the blessings"

Jessica Care Moore is on the front line, be it on the stage of the Apollo, a bar, cafe, public class room, lecture hall, college campus or street. A daughter of Nikki Giovanni, Sonia Sanchez, June Jordan, Jayne Cortez, Ntozake Shange, Amiri Baraka, Gil Scott Heron and The Last Poets (to name a few), she has found her own voice among dynamic poets of her generation such as Paul Beatty, Asha Bandele, Willie Perdomo, Ruth Forman, Edwin Torres, Ras Baraka and Kevin Powell, to name a published few. Hailing out of Detroit, with The Words Don't Fit

in My Mouth under her own publishing house, Moore Black Press, she also fol-
lows in the tradition of some our most important poetic movers and shakers—
all publishers; all working from a working class perspective—Dudley Randall
(Broadside Press), Naomi Long Madget (Lotus Press), and Melba Joyce Boyd
(formerly an editor at Broadside, now with her own press, Past Tents).

Like Jayne Cortez before her, this is her mouth on paper, her heart on her
sleeves, her refusal to shut the fuck up and swallow her silence.

This book may be a bottle of black girl juice upside your head or something
to curl up with in bed while listening to the rain against your window.

Tony Medina
Editor, Poet and Professor

TWO

Detroit girls make you remember that life is made up of minutes and you gotta spend them like you're happy with your purchases. I'm happy with the time I spent with Jessica because she makes me remember that we, as a people, have dried out our senses in order to "maintain". She makes me remember because she pours water on all of those senses and makes everybody ALIVE.

ALIVE we are when we sit in poetry readings, laughing at the snooty girls and the "artier than thou" cult members. ALIVE we are when we sit on the train, spotting all the tall cute men this New York City has to offer. (We Detroit girls go for those brothas who cause attention!). ALIVE we are when we cry during "Set It Off" because we saw our girls from Detroit on that screen-not believing they will be alive in five years-while munching movie popcorn and calling our rare excursion a "vacation." We are key in each other's support because we know where each other has come from. 3-1-3. Detroit. What!??!
Stage or no stage, there will still be late night phone calls on the trials and tribulations of being black women artists and what that means to our rent and our sex life. I will still rub my heart when I hear "Who Will Be The Last Poet" or hear my name in "I Bet You Want Me to Write Fiction." It was her words that got me through producing my first Off-Off Broadway play because she made me realize that I was in the midst of making the impossible happen (chaos, I call it) and I, of all people, could do it. If she didn't insist that the world was crazy for not being open to all of the bomb, unheard of writers and people blowing up the spot and putting their footprint on the world (it seems like Black folks ain't allowed to leave legacies), I would swear that we did all this work for ourselves. In any case, when your sistergirl is your only indulgence while you're on a mission to make the impossible happen, then you wanna spend your minutes with Jessica.

T. Tara Turk
Playwright

THREE

A lot of people are wondering "Who is Jessica Care moore?" The best way for me to tell you who she is, is to tell what she is not. Jessica is not a feminist. She is not a bohemian. She is not a nationalist. She is not a revivalist. She is not a hip hop poet. She is not an African deity. She is not a model, or, a Revlon spokesperson. She is not Tiger Woods. Jessica Care Moore is a terribly gifted poet from Detroit, Michigan-who is doing what all greats do in their fields. She is elevating the game beyond the small cafes of trendy Downtown Brooklyn; Beyond the tiny insular clicks of the "cultural" community and its "figures" in their action hero poses.

Beyond the pomp and ceremony of the "scene", Jessica is knocking down the walls of the opium dens in this distant, not quite residential district of town called poetry.Walls that have too long been the sounding board of a cautious few afraid to move forward because they fear a future that may not include their names on the marquee. (Oh drats!) Reaching out beyond the minions of the dormantly hip and tres chic, Jessica has decided that there are a few OTHER people out there who could use some "touchin". Namely, everyone. Jessica is not sleeping. Jessica is not confused. Jessica is not afraid. Jessica Care Moore is here. Pay attention.

Dante Beze a.k.a Mos Def
Actor and Emcee

DETROIT READ

Four

I am the flame cracklin in a Sunday newspaper
Stick bon fire on Detroit's west side
blues songs strum along pink and yellow candy necklaces
Held together by white string turning into blue collar for hire
I am a convertible green cadillac
And my hair don't blow straight
Belle Isle park and panten leather Adidas
Shine my seven-and- a-half foot fetish for Black top
I'm 24 and trying to stop writing these poems
about home. . .

These words are Detroit Red words. Are Alabama, English, French, African and blue collar. These words are young on Friday, old and wise on Monday. These are love words, painful words, beautiful words, cussing words, nasty words, ugly words, truthful words, sincere words, confident words, my words, somebody else's words, make you wanna dance words, cause sometimes there are no words to describe making love to a sunset, the rage of an oppressed people, the taste of my ma's macaroni and cheese, a woman's touch, unborn babies, a ride through Belle Isle in the summer,
The sound of Hip Hop at the Rhythm Kitchen
Sweat on the walls of the music institute
A 7-year old saying she's a poet too
There are no words that can capture the summer of `89
My West Side posse, my people on the East. The Black student organizations who forced WSU to closed classes to celebrate the Martin Luther King Jr. Holiday.
Sometimes there are no words for winning, losing, fighting, bleeding, needing. No words to describe Kwame Toure's smile, Malcolm's laugh or Assata's spirit. Sometimes there are no words to explain the honor of the Apollo stage. The gift the audience gives. The feeling when you read your first Haki poem or hear Sonia Sanchez bless the mic, while Nikki Giovanni whispers revolution into your conscience. Words can't always express how it feels to buy Adidas to wear to a Run D-M-C concert, sometimes words aren't great enough, strong enough, or proud enough to cry cause your daddy never had a chance to tell the folks at all the Detroit truck stops,
"That's my baby on TV." No words to properly pronounce I love you too or

tell you I see you in the front row. Words aren't always fearless enough to say my English momma introduced me to Lorraine Hansberry, Walker and Angelou. Words don't always fit into the prison of language, can't always get lifted by a 40 ounce of black girl juice, but these are simply my words, holy spit water making flowers grow in the projects, children laugh, wetting the mouths of those thirsty for liberation, screaming for a voice for everyday people, speaking backwords in order to move For Word Ashay, Sharrif, this is still a movement.

THE FIRST POEM IN THE BOOK

I am the next jessica Care moore poem
nicknamed ungodly
a long way from home and maybe my baby
will stop me from rhyming
my mind's eye keeps crying
trying to please those opinions
running like snotty nose/wrapping my b-girl ponytail with torn brown panty-
hose/hiding heaven's halos inside human ha-choos and hiccups/I am awk-
ward angel tangled between streets that frown my smile so now I cuss
loud/It's my daddy's trait/guess I'm a tom girl/It was his first name/blame
the tight braids for all the headaches/teaching me nothing was their first mis-
take/I am awake now/check my footprints/sent to save niggas/I walk with
switches/wear out my shoes quick/kick and scream to live my dreams/my
voice is low/keep my head high/despite the shoot downs/months get dizzi-
er/It's a sign of womanhood/I have no time for men-tal pause/I want my own
pill/kill the noise/I write poetic obituaries for my boys/you'll never know
them/hope they can hear me now/swim cross 14 stiches and scars/In a world
where little girls drive cadillac cars/stars don't sink their footprints in my
cement back/gets walked on by motown legends/my world is smokey/I can't
inhale right/my lungs lack fresh air/I live down the street from city parks and
re-creations/hide my head inside books and wool skullies/you must be a
school girl/shake my smile off/I'm from the westside/enjoy men tall like my
five brothers/hustler spirit/just can't help myself/new and improved niggas
bring the corny lines/hang with a crew without gang signs/It was an addic-
tive love/didn't recognize the real war/take a bullet and abandon my own crib
if I have to/I was living in the projects/didn't have an address there/It's where
my jumper got hot/got to find a deeper

cause/applause are unknown now/platforms are shoes/In news I pay
dues/write my way up/way out/poetry becomes my paintbrush/rush to
school still/will my girls die in the crossfire?/warriors rent my body at their
disposal
where are my weapons?
I am alone now.

black coals waiting to turn to diamond/It seems bad timing keeps me lying in my bed/lying to myself/trying to stop rhyming/steady climbing/there I go again/can't conquer mountain tops/an occasional fine man will make my pen stop/throw an american dream inside my backpack/lock my doors/I survive a carjack/threw 2 my keys/got on knees/asked the bright-eyed brotha not to blow my head off/he let me keep my cowrie shell rings

3

This is my brotha This my brotha

4

I don't believe my own rhetoric

5

I told him I got shit to do/air to breathe/now he's a flashback at close range/I hear the clicking/see the michigan snow fall/I crawl inside and write my first poem.

6

The mutha fucka stole my pen

I bet you want me to write fiction

I could paint my front porch green
Smile through my teeth so I didn't seem so mean
Give you a glass of water so you could swallow my reality
Without Guilt
Warm your heart
Spend time showing you how to sew up the holes of my
African Quilt
Guess I could write a thesis on why I write
With Black dialect or diction
I bet you want me to write fiction

Cause you can't handle my truth!

You want novellas that tella pretend made up existence
With fairies
When I fly without wings on the weekend
And you want me to wear a costume on stage
Depict a fictionary tale that deals with Black rage
On an island far far away
On a planet no one's every heard of
Want me to chop off my female into
Carefully constructed chapters
With titles like Snow Black and my seven boys
Or Mary had just a little ham
But I don't own shiny red shoes and
the green witch melted
So when you read my work you felt it

Now you want me to write fiction
With happy endings
Typical beginnings
Want to imagine my existence
Is a figment of your twisted imagination
With lots of exhaling and no breathing
You want a black women's story bout how she's so alone
But I got a good man at home
Think I can't compete with those who test my black power temperature

With panting wet dog tongues
You think I'm too young to have a relevant truth
You want to paint my experience in bright pastels
As if my brown world is lacking color
And you want me to speak to my audience
Lying on my back
On top of a long Black couch
As publishers posing as psychologists
Analyze my analogies and antonyms
Trying to figure our where the hell I've been

But Black women don't have time for therapy!

You want to marry ketchup with my blood
Too thick
Pouring so slow drops of my watered-down life
So you can enjoy a glass of BlackGirl Juice
With your morning paper without choking
You want me to write fiction
So then there's no way of connecting my words
something tangible
Down the road you can write me off
Calling my characters fictional
Their lives false
My afro grows too thick to please the animated cartoon
You've outlined in one-dimensional crayons
Representing a generation without a last name
Building wooden tables of continents
Take a velium
This is only my first
And there are others like me
I have their phone numbers and bra sizes
And the fact is your fiction can't be created without my blues print
Dipped in fresh Black ink
Cause this poem is real
And if you're really afraid
Why are you here?
At the end of my poems life
And she doesn't commit suicide
She survives

With a wicked smile
And the story never ends cause my girl T.Tara Turk said
In real life nothing ever does
And I believe her
Writing her way out of fiction

Sitting on a green porch in Harlem recreating the spirit of
A women named Sugar
Ain't our reality a sweet thing
A taste you can't seem to place
Can't pretend not to know
But we exist
Yes we do
It's a fact.

BLACK COALS WITH DIAMOND HEARTS

For Charlotte/Lynn/Trea/Angie/Alexis/Nikki/and
all my Detroit dogs.

What will they name us?
After we lie our bodies across the East and West Side divide
That swerves with motown myth and low ride grips down 7 miles
Of no where to go streets

Gotta get my degree my car my house my man
my life together
But today I gotta bury him again
Pretend I don't know them   friends
moms wants to know why nice girls pin up Michigan's Most Wanted
On the fridge under the yellow butterfly magnets

Match the curtains Match the description

We've dented car hoods with imaginary high heels
During Piston playoffs   our daddy's play golf
Bad Boys were good ole days
Sometimes pissing outside is o.k.
The apple jack used to slip down with ignorant ice
Rolling after-hour red dice with somebody else's money
Suicide ruins the joy rides of drive by blood smeared
On our front porches
We simply keep brothas alive   silent sexy torches
Blowing fire into existence inhaling bullet proof wind
Ready for verbal war or a country cuss word
World news calls us a ghost town still I walk among old eyes
Pouring southern comfort on truck stop pancakes
that play numbers
Sixties riots still burn down homes in 1997
boarded up ashes, fire and black bottom dreams
committed suicide a long time ago
I see Malcolm walking down Woodward
Martin in Hart Plaza
And they don't recognize this chocolate city anymore
I've watched tears crawl back into our eye sockets

Without any time to cry we pray this time we won't die
When the club lets out
Holding long kisses wishing we could
tongue down any man who's gentle
Or recognizes the feminine underneath the westside hat
Somehow see my 7-mile switch as graceful

Never say goodbye to my cousin Lynn
Smiling back black spirit child
Got African drums under her white feet
Strong heart screams lit up 24 hour Coney Island parking lot
Your sicilian french blood was safe with me

I could protect you because I was down with the
brothas from the Eastside who drove monte carlos with
tinted windows
Or an Impala with a 350 engine
We built in the backyard

Almost took you and Nikki out with ego crushed bullets
Entering at close range through the drivers side window
This is a night out for nice girls with chicken winged
Wish Bones in their pockets
Ringing out dirty water from grounded clouds that fog our forever
Burning night smoke out of love sick lungs
Washing our feet with homegirl holy water
Store owners Speak arabic in our ears that smell of green meat and month old
bread repackaged and resold to our intelligence
Sticking bright neon orange three for a dollar signs on our heads
Another one of my boys is shot dead
For stealing a five cent tangy taffy

We are lawyers, journalists, business executives, poets, philosophers, activists,
hypocrites and confused
Intelligent hoodlums who hide dime bags in sweat socks
High off of the scent of new shoes cadillac cars and
Men who dress better than we do
Conscience of everything
Believers in fast paced dreams

We Detroit, We sistas, We Rosa, We Protest, We Laugh,
We Belle Isle, We Supreme, We Wonder, We Smokey,
We "booty shaking music," We Mid-west flavor, We country
We lay face down on warm cement
Pretending not to run after buses
Waving our tranfers in the air hoping they will take us
Where we think we've always wanted to go
Detroit girls wait for the black sun rising
To turn young hot coals back to diamonds

Rising of the Sun

Without yeast it still rises in the east
Sets at a half past peace
White doves humbly fly low chocolate-dipped wings
Saving planets Roses romantic
I like the little soft red things
Bring me the wilted brown stems
I want to marry them
Brooklyn dust wipes
It's dirt at my door
My heart is cornrolled so my chest itches with urges
Undeserved eyes watch balanced baby making hips
Running with warrior heat guns
Getting a strong grip of sun-filled grenades
Brushing sweat from our brows
Girls just want to have fun
We wake with earthquakes
Morning dew falls from our waterbreaks
Fertilizing wild weeds growing through
Cemented city streets
Green baby feet growing in gardened ghettoes
Smiling flower children
Throwing tomatoed ammunition at brick built
To bury ambition
Silence oral tradition
Screaming lullabies our lungs learning to laugh
On behalf of bruised brilliance
Can you feel this?
Close your eyes so you can see us
Riding our rhythm till sky falls
Residuals won't be rewarded
You cannot imitate our royalties

Sun stroked I swim through day blues
Holding tight to night dreams
And they all come true
Cause I blinked twice switched hard
Twisted my neck left
Tongue kissing crescent moonlight
The sun eclipses on my lips
I am a hot kiss
Salt water saliva sips swallowing seas
Washing the ash off wise knees
Forgetting to stand up dust off
And fly   now and then
Extend my natural bend that sends music
Sliding down curves of crooked spinal cords
Teaching the offbeat to dance
Spineless to speak writers to walk what they write
Sightless visions look legitimate to wide-eyed followers
Searching for tomorrow is today
So set your watch to never stop at red lights
It's why we're walking in circles
My back be a bridge to boogie wonderland
In a woman's hands
You can hear Billie laughing
Celebrating her own holiday everyday
Pulling harp strings from her gut
What but extreme pleasure pushes pain to surface
It is the ride of an oceans wave before it reaches the shore
Helping vocal cords roar and ring

Believe in small insignificant things

Chocolate fire wings light up the atmosphere
Soaring through sunshine
As fearless brown angels sleep
Poetry be my angel wings
So I get the Holy ghost
from all the blessings

Watch the Water

Brown heads protected by Afro puff cloud pillows
Silhouettes be getting jealous
Throwing rocks at our unreachable windows
Blending with darkness
Swimming in moonlit skywater
We race time carrying our past
In our peripheral sight
Riding candy apple red schwin bikes
Running hot water
Desert daughters
Quenching unworthy thirsts
We swallow our spirits
Blowing life into clear liquid embryo bubbles
And we don't pop!
And we don't pop!
Stop super-imposing super model stomachs
On our mental screens
Flat is out
Curved queens make brothas fiend
Seen flying without wings
Sings Sara Vaughn cutting the lawn
Yawns rain-bowed halos
In desert hood storms, warns of the war to come
Camouflaged in headwraps and Hip Hop gear
Fearless female hearts bleed
Taking firebullets driving by to steal her new seeds
Feeds future friendly fire next door
When mommas left them home alone
Magic fingertips got granddaddy green thumb
Growing garden flowers in the snow
Nobody knows why our rhythm walks on ice
Cool sistas shooting dice delivering diamonds
Down under thunders that sound
Making your head nod
Robbed thighs showing some leg
Hitchhiking rides on freedom trains
Silk skinned grinning as it rains
Can't explain why you cannot surf on our web sites
Looking at you like yea right!

Our waves remember how you computed polluted plans
Reducing rivers and oceans
With royal hands and stolen lands
We watched from night sky niles
Smiled as suffocation choked our water-blue
daughters
Our cocoa color creates the muddy water
Returning to shore with earth tones
Baptized by brilliance
Sun babies bathe in honey-mustard glow
Running 360 degree circles around Bermuda Triangles
Sticking in the inside of lost toes
Traveling on shores they feel they somehow know
Dust daughters discover dance
Mystery and music beneath the mud
And when we're in a dirty mood
We'll drown you with our flood.

Rainbows Baby Rainbows

(for my London crew: Malika B. - Jonzi D. - Mallissa Read & Paul)

I run combat-booted through water puddles
Wishing we could cuddle
Leaving my reflection in wet footsteps
Trying to catch me pouring 25 raindrops
On my head
They keep falling
Liquid slides off my pain proof skin licking itself dry
With my hot-mouth tongue
Young and numb fingered
Pointing becomes pointless

As crowds pass in the other un-annointed direction
Sectioned I shallow through emotional showers
Hot-cold-warm turns
Now water burns third degree confusion
And they call it higher education

Keep a smile on my face
Cause my inkwell always has the blues
Bucket-fulls of dreams
Echo from the black bottom of yesterdays you
Didn't forget why there's
So many soooonngs about rainbooowws
Wearing Kangoled halos and baggy jeans
Hot angel wings fly   set fire

Burning roofs off mouth canals
That snail across multi-colored light arches
In search of a pot of mold

When gold-souls travel lines
Carved inside starved calm palms
Patiently waiting with paper-plated hope
For a little portion of food for thought
But we're all too scientific
We smell bullshit and call it manure
Sure eyes turn blurry and curried

Information is spicy and hurried
And no one really "gets it" anymore
Cracks in the door leave my heart sore
So now it only opens for special occasions

burning sensations or the sound of a five heartbeat temptation

Sometimes I wish that raindrops would fall

You lie —awake
Speaking sleepy untruths
Awake-walking
Sleep-talking
And now I'm bored with the mental workout
2-3-4
Socialist

Still I voted for Clinton-Gore?

What happens when 3 are in love?
Breaking ice   and bread   cold sand
Witch got hard walking down the aisle south feet
Broomstick dust in your newlywed

You overheard all the good stuff I said
Bout getting our sylllables in bed?
So we can SOUUNNDD out the meaning of our relation
Ship our spirits to a free nation
Say I do

Release oxygen filled balloons .
That bust before spelling out all the answers
Over - our - heads
And you know nothing   stupid again
Cause you didn't bother to ask if I wanted to
Drown float splash doggy paddle or dance
In your bath?

Us water women who save slave waves
With star fish kiss
Hiding the magic of romance
Between their rainbow hips
Switching between the dry space
Inside sky tears
Wetting the non-believers for years
Deaf ears couldn't hear me
Crying at your window sill

Loud musical taps
Drip dropping my pain
Hitting the wind at half-mast
Remember how you'd ask
Me to wet you up like water hose when fully clothed
Exposing the naked color of
Who you really are   between your muddy toes

Dirty and unsure

I'm always watching you watching me from below
Next time you hear my waters let go

Check for the rainbows baby   the rainbows

Less-Home

cardboard boxes

that you carry

from the alley

just to move to

your new place

are so meaningful to me

if you could imagine

living here, inside,
i don't think
you'd take away my

home

with a grin on your face
and a key
in your pocket

There are no asylums for the
real crazy women

For Vivienne

T.S. Eliot is a english tea drinking dog
Who quietly and without remorse
Stole his wife's spirit
Threw it in a closet
And never returned
He fed her just enough inspiration
To help him write his next poem
Took her sanity and said goodbye
Dragged her dignity across polished silver
Ate her ambitions aborted her thoughts of motherhood
All in the name of literary recognition
Poets owe a debt to those who's lives we put on the page
T.S. Eliot, Anglo nerd knight of the canon kings
Your spine is a weak book binder held together with stolen titles, old glue and
shame
Does anybody care about Vivienne?
You loved him unconditionally even after he put you in that crazy house
Vowed he was the greatest writer to live until your death
Wrap his books in cheap saran wrap and burn the words
With your bra sister!
He stole vowels from your tongue, heart and nervous muscles
Drop your cigarette ashes on the shiny black typewriter
Spill a drink on his desk, drink the ink from his pens
It's your blood anyway
Rebel Vivienne!
Read his poems the way he wish he could
Bring them life

It's your life on display in all those paragraphs anyway
Vivienne there are no asylums for the real crazy women!
There are no asylums for the real crazy women!
Cause none of my girls are there

But there is a prison where spirit thieves are shook
From their skin
Still, in your after life, I know you will fight for him
And never tarnish his distinguished name
But your love for the truth of a poets eyes
Blinks not the same

Afro *Dances* by Candlelight

Orange flowers rose from AFRO crowned candles
Mahogany waxed women making men melt
With flickers of light
Leading the land of the lost to candyland
Sand shadows make the night dirty
As we wash guilt from our skin
Sleepwalk till day comes and bees hum
Before we wake from scorpion sting
We've killed our kings forgive us our sins
Our modern laws are written in number 2 pencils
Erase mulitple choice mistakes justified because
We're only human
That shit doesn't count anymore
At war with the seven-hundred century old
Cushite warrior whispering wise words
I've never read
In this lifetime

Death clocks keep the hours close
Most men ignore unconscious voices
Until gun shot loud american- made- violence beats
On the skin of young ear drums dying before day is dark
And daddy's hung we sung with blackbird lungs
Wrapping our blue skies inside pupiled lies that look at us
With one eye open
Hoping to gain some understanding
From comfortable   distances Forever reliving past instances

We are flesh-covered conscious spirits homeless I guess
Hallucinating how heaven must feel at high noon
I dare stare downs with sunlight
Kickin' up star dust with dirt bikes

Just want a chance to walk the wings of a fly jet
Nose dive into copper sunsets
Light a match allow my body to dance
Among the flames

Then freeze the frame perfect as picture might
Lady of illuminated light
Raindrops stand still drying on our Cherokee cheeks
Undeniable gifts await the meek who speak less
Everyone's got a story to tell when the fire gets hot
Questions of believe it or not
Never
Innocence pushed off the edge of forever
Natural blazes blow show human hands raising
Standing gun powder-gazed
Big guilty fingers glow in the dark
Still candle children survive two sets of boy girl twins
Holding the heat of truthful light

Leading the way back to candy land
Is a mother's smiling wounded wax heart.

Don't you hate when people ask you stupid questions?
for paul beatty

I saw Nelson Mandela walking past Burger King in London
Drinking a vanilla milkshake
Lactose lakes overflow as my belly plays an acoustic guitar
Out of tune   by mistake

Searching for the darkest South African Star
So I can get a bigger picture
A brighter mixture of miracle-swirled Ice-cream cones
The trucks just don't
come around here
anymore
It's safer to lick the wind
People ask why it matters where my people been
My life is summed up in a break beat
A semi-sweet half chocolate existence
Melting in my mouth so I think through hopeful hands
Aspire to change the rhythm of any land

My spirit crossed over three lifetimes ago
So it's hard for me to talk slow
Live pretending there's not more to know
Then this foreign neighborhood
I've been born again Into
concrete catholic Kodak college killings
Glass ceilings
god willing
I'll still keep some feeling left in my taste-budding tongue
Singing songs memorized when Motown was young
And dinner was a group thing

Pushing in   Pushing out
My body is on it's own twisted route
Running away from Ronald McDonald trumps
Who believe they can really buy the earth
As if man knows soils true worth

Forced to pay for our liquid gift
Through kitchen sinks
Virginia trees choked by unfamiliar rope wrapped
Around its nocturnal neck
That hasn't woke up yet
Doesn't want the leaves to see
How we destroy humanity
I ordered a coke and fries
Five extra pounds for a packet of smashed tomatoes

While it's snowing in Soweto
I'm jogging through Johannesburg
Flying over Ghana on a ghetto-ized Sankofa bird
Heard BigBen was just another overweight man
Who doesn't know how to dance in time

A british woman asked why Black people in America
Feel they need to go back to Africa when they weren't
Born   Over
THERE?

We exchanged a silent stare

I hear there's a new veggie whopper on the menu!
I answered
Peering out the window watching a beautiful thing
Nelson and Winnie Mandela
Walking right past Burger King
Drinking vanilla milkshakes

Don't you think it's time we finally ate?

I'm Done Dating D-J's

I'm done waiting around at the end of the night
as the club clears for the very last time
I'm done being the supportive sista willing to hear your latest
craziest track chime.
I have NO more requests
Take me off the guest list
Before I have a fit!
I'm pretending like it was a mirage.
How's it feel to sabotage someone's heart
and sample the sound on a new track.
Musical Heart Attack.
I'm tired of conversations at the club where you spin
Vibing about the world.
Fake People and Jinns.
No more saying yes to late night invitations to listen.
Wishing.

You were putting ME on wax.
Throwing my heart-beat in your headphones.
So, you'll never be alone.
A loving lyric, If you payed attention you would hear it
No more sitting at the sidelines
Laying my heart and soul on your turntables
So you're able
To create a fate you're afraid to recognize
D-J's with closed eyes is a cute trick.
But it's wic-wic- wacked
As you concentrate on your Bobcat
To ignore a sista that's got your back.
We're a perfect blend.
Don't flex.
Cause I can make you flutter.
Sound smooth like melted butter.

I'm done riding your WHEELS OF STEEL
Won't tell me how you feel.
I admire your passion, trying to make
cash and you blend is truly tight.
But I kept you warm through the night.
Don't know what you're cuing or doing
with your "phat" party mix.
On stage doing tricks.
I never gave you ultimatums

You gave me your crate of records
And I played them.
Hey, Mr. D-J with your trunk full of
vinyl.
This song is final.
You've lost the light in your
better days.
I'm done dating D-J's.

Half/white revolutionary rain dance

I bit down on soft pink lips and allowed the blood to drip over my chin
Cause I thought the red-bone
Thin-Lipped kisses
I didn't ask for
Would swell up
Like puffy eyes
And disappear
Into dust daughters
Dating white men
Who could relate
To my love for
Karen Carpenter
Assuming Hip Hop
Was just an unwanted urge
An unnecessary twitch in my neck
Brushing through breaking ends
Connecting me with my daddy's kin
Dipped in Caramel Syrup
And cocoa butter candies
Lands me jobs in
Colored Colonized pieces of
Africa
In America
Daily Affirmations of light-water flushed face
Race hollow bits of bone white
Will make you wish your skin turned
Inside out
Confused you camaflouge
Mixed feelings of me
But revolution resuscitates
My name
During rain dances
And I keep the beat
Just fine
Cause revolution resuscitates
My name
During rain dances
And I keep the beat
Just Fine

But revolution resuscitates
My name
During rain dances
And I keep the beat
Just fine
Cause revolution resuscitates
My name
During rain dances
And I keep the beat
Just Fine
Until ugly images of what made me
Interrupts your conscious thinking
Much madness moves your mouth mumbling
Slave terms
Like mullato
Melting pots burn hot black handles
Lit by Light candles
But I've seen Blacker
Tones of Night
Reflecting Bougie suits
Sewn too tight
Breaking Bread
Airborne
With comrades
Of white flight
There are Africans
Who don't trust
Your revolutionary Yankees
Yellow Yo-Yo's
Got no where to go
But Black
Biting hard on my tongue
As you tied up my totality
Cutting my spirit in half
Forming hateful words
An aching douse
What's the difference
Between the cotton fields and
Being raped, bare back in the house?
Noose knotted tightly around

Half-white niggas
Red-blood splashed on southern nape
Guess your family tree
Escaped.
Hope to not see you on the frontin' lines
When war whispers to warriors
Wearing Black-water-colored
War paint
It's time
Cause revolution
Resuscitates my name
During rain dances
And I keep the beat
Just fine.

My daddy's soul-music 2/14/97

She sang at my soul with rose thorn throat. Gave gladys grace, felt her in a special space. Held dirty plastic bags close to her breast like I hold pillows when I'm alone. She broke into an aretha rift. Sang with skinny lips. She kidnapped me on a midnight train to georgia, and I continued rocking my head as she rocked her body to an Al Green high note. The one that makes your spine curl up inside its self, wishing it could walk straight, but still knows one leg was born with a slow sexy drag that could never catch up with the other. I didn't know the A train stopped there, but when the door opened, my music was playing so loudly my soul was forced into the heart of Madison, Alabama. I took the flowers from her curly hair, placed them in her into my daddy's soil. Planted music under my skin. Above his grave. Watering my grounded feet with pisces tears allowing me to part and walk along cemented rivers without fear.

It's been three years and I still want to celebrate your birthday, when I know you never wanted to grow that old. And as I board plane after plane I wonder why the only time we flew together was when they were transporting you back down south. I had to travel alone, knowing I couldn't point out the clouds, share a bag of peanuts or remind you that smoking is not allowed. Today as I write my poetry I know you laugh at the music they connect our work with, when you gave life to the second to last daughter of your soul music. Only gravity can hold my body down when Marvin moans " my mistake," and I dream It's me singing back. You know it was, baby! I answer my phone every night before I go to bed, pretending your calling to tell me you love me for the last time. I want to tell the woman to shut up and stop singing to me in your voice. Quite reminding me of all the road trips we took with the supremes, and stories about how you used to take them to get their hair done. We drove between the mountains, and left our initials in the wind with the top down. My mouth moves with her words and rotting teeth, and I wonder how this down south girl ended up singing alone on a New York City train.

Then I wonder who the hell I was talking to. Singing with. Since no one else is around but you, and we both got weak teeth. Then I grab your obituary and promise to memorize the names of my grandparents we never met. Annie Mae Gilliam and Berry Lee Moore. Damn, those some old country names. Yea. This is the stop where I get off. And that woman with the black teeth, she just keeps on laughing and singing right through me.

Black Bums From the Bible

I know I just saw Noah
driving a 1967 ark!
His skin was brown like bark
and he was tall like a tree.
I'd love to swing
or just sing a church hymn.
or watch him play ball in the gym.
I never sweat the feel of sweat
At least not with him yet.
Met him in another life?
Was I his warrior wife?
Bouncing hydraulics, makes my stomach sick
So, he slowed down his ride, and adjusted the stickshift.

Yeah, that's better.
I remember every thread in his sweater
Cause I know no matter what the weather
Noah, like the post man, always delivers!
Together we would sail down rough, red rivers
And come up for air only to breathe in some fresh truth.
I know what all those history school teacher told us
But I swear my brothas: Sharrif, Will, Khary, Pharoah, and Ken, look just like
Moses!
We pulled up to Coney Island. Just order some hot fries, please hold the ham
When I saw this brotha come stumbling toward me,
and I swear he was Abraham
Except his breath was kickin out that liquid promoted by
Uncle Sam
Damn, was this Lynwood, Flatbush, or the cradle of civilization?
Without hesitation.
I felt an overwhelming obligation to give that old brotha
a few coins, and a comb for his long gray beard.
In the hood, he's the one most feared.
Now I know why
Bums are angels sent down from the sky.
To pay homage to mother earth, in dirty pants, and
old plaid shirts.

A walking bible on Prospect Park or Belle Isle
Straight white teeth that sometimes smiled
Was this all just a dream?
From my girl came a scream
Cause the weather outside was about to freeze us.
But before we made it to the car, we saw the prophet Jesus.
Just getting up from a nap in a cardboard box
Asking for a spare dime!
With no watch to tell time.
But he always had some wine to drink.
Kinda makes you think.
Into the party store walked Cain and Able

This stop on the block was better than any of Aesop's Fables.
And how does one know who's a prophet and who ain't?
Just don't rub off like paint
Being a black Saint
He can climb down my chimney any day!
And deliver a sack full of knowledge for a glass of
purified water and some ginger root.
Black brotha from the scriptures wearing loose jeans
and black boots
Smelling like imported oils.
Found on the tip of the Himalayas
I can feel the energy from my boyz Ismael and Isiah.
Anointing my soul
Spiritual and Serene.
For this type of mental stimulation many conscious sistas fiend.
Straight from the bible and the Quran
On every level, he's making my mind-state complete.
No shoes on his feet.
He's got long dreads down his back, cause he never cuts his hair
Next time you walk past, don't ignore his blood-shot stare.
Don't you dare be afraid to give him a moment of conversation
Together you may find a way to end the homeless situation
And you may even fall in love.
With a black man from heaven
America labels a bum.

Breeze
dedicated to Thomas Davis Moore

I felt a strong breeze pass through and I knew it was you.
It had an attitude and as it traveled it fussed about getting my oil
changed, and smiled an angel's grin.

Told me having babies wasn't a sin, but don't you dare!
That breeze taught me things in school I'd never learn.
Like how to get home on the side streets to save gas I'd always burn.

That breeze was bad, a survivor, teaching me how to survive.
So, I know his spirit will always live.

That breeze kept going, blowing, no matter what he'd never give.

His smile lit up his face when he talked about his kids
In the truck stops and corner coneys he made sure he always did.

That breeze loved Temptations songs, so in his car we'd sing-a-long.
Now those Motown hits sound more like sadder songs.

That breeze carried loads on his trucks and on his back.
Wearing sunglasses in the summertime
Sportin' a convertible white leather interior Cadillac.

Get your lesson, insisted the wind - my smart mouth twin.

My boy, my road partner, that breeze was my best friend.
I can't wait until the day that breeze passes through me once again.

Saying Goodbye to that strong breeze is something I'll probably never
do, but will i say to my Daddy, with all my heart, "I loved you, too."

Your Daughter,

Jess

Tribal Scars

Urban rights of passage
Smashed to dust
Disappear into darkness
Turning into big willie dippers
Twinkle Twinkle little star
How I wonder how you go
Where you are?
Just to get your tribal scar
No time to talk about the Mau Mau
Cause the Now Now
Keeps claiming our babies too soon
Why ya wanna fly to the moon?
When you got your own Black planet
Looking into the rearview
See yourself
And you can't stand it
See the foggy water
Still we drink it
Link it to oceans of 40s
You've poured out for
Dead homies
Stiff bodies sinking above water
You say you did it for your daughter
Make it alone
That's what you taught her
Rights of passage
Is now a slaughter
Sexy kissable cuts stitched
On brown stomach
Traveling railroad tracks
Cho-Choing down   black skin
Is sacrificial
Initial reaction
Scorpio satisfaction
Some say it's even cute
What's a pretty scar
Doing on a face like you

An angel touched me
A brotha cut me

Stuck me during a hustle
Gotta prove we strong
How long ago you got yours?
Who gave you your stripes?
Ripe raw splits
Bloody fists
Missed your mama
At the last burial
Show me yours
I'll show you mine
Filled with obituaries scary still shots
Look a lot like senior year
Without fear b-boys walk down
One way streets in hoods-man
Sway heads to sampled beats
As an African boy proves his man-hood
Would you give up your smooth tissue
International lovers mac daddy G-Q's
Never knew
There was something greater than a
Ghetto moon permanent night light up blunts
So we philosophize about what we want
Can't go out like no punk
Keeping it real
Yea, I believe in tooth fairies too
Cool fools protect tribe territory
Glory without God-owns the earth
Fighting over dirt-don't belong to you
Slit your veins blow out your own peoples veins
Got a bullet lodged behind your ear
Sometimes it's hard to hear
Hard-core covered in decorative warrior gear
Maasi girls wouldn't undergo
Transitions into womanhood for

Cowards like you
Showing off war scars earned on the same block
From the same tribe
Slightly raised bats bullets and blades
Rights of passage for African American slaves
Cradle to grave
I gotta get mine
You gotta yours

People say it adds character
So, where were you at?
Suprised.
Nobody in line to get circumcised
But you got this phat scar during last nights
Drive by?
Why you wanna wear green camouflage?
Ain't no trees here
The shit ain't going down in central park
Just wear black
Hide from yourself!
But you don't have the heart
Claiming you a street scribe
Stabbing up the bodies of your own tribe
Why you wanna rush to get to the moon?
Trying you be a temporary superstar
Hey baby, how'd you get that scar?
An angel touched me
Ancestors drew blood
Marks that made us free
Proved who be for real Nobody died
No one was killed feel one long swipe
Under brown eyes gently placed above
Cheek bone
Didn't get my 14 stitches in the name of posse,
Click, west or east side crew
I got it at home.

excuse me...

if i fall in love
with the thought of YOU and I.
excuse me if you don't agree with the
thought of you and me.
if you touched me,
i would melt inside,
the tender thoughts
of subtle sighs,
that kill the souls of lovers lost
and
dictionary meanings of this thing called
love.
help me now,
before the fall.
i'm sorry dear,
if i've been wrong,
and made your smiles
go away.
excuse me if it's not right
for wanting you to stay.
i think
i'm in love with the thought
of finding,
but i'm afraid
it's my emotions i will hide.
excuse me if i fall in love
with just the thought-
of
you
and
i.

X Chromosome

Dreaded locks. Sweat socks. Tied up boots.
Working hard to make a way.
Brotha, it's gonna be okay.
To me, you can always come home.
Y?
I'm your X chromosome
Soft Oils. Clean Sheets. We were supposed to meet
Making love mentally. Brotha some day we'll both be free
Outside yourself you'll never have to roam
I'm your better half.
Your backbone.
I'm your X chromosome.
Strong hands, comforting, controlling my cravings, even when you're misbehaving
I can't wait until you break a smile
Baggy jeans, or Armani suit, I just love your style.
6'5 with an attitude, 5'9 and you cook exotic foods
Fabulous. You make my eyes water, my mouth foam.
I love you.
 Y?
 Cause I'm your X Chromosome.
And since you started off first with my female gene,
I just like the way you wear your jeans!
Don't like to play games with my mind.
Understand why other women fight for what's genetically,
biologically, and emphatically mine
as well give up, cause he only wants black coffee in his cup
Brotha, I never want to be your ex -X.
Cause you're my perfect fit.
I just like the way you sit.
Next to me and hold on to me like you do
Black men have that non-chalant cool
That drives us X-Chromosomes crazy, and after making love, makes us lazy.
I love it when you open my door and call me dear.
Brotha, you'll never have anything or anyone to fear.

I love it when you open my door and call me dear
Brotha, you'll never have anything or anyone to fear

Cause your X Chromosome's black and she's got your back.
Inside my body, you'll always have a home.
Y ask Y?
I'm just your X Chromosome.

This is not a poem about revolution

Dedicated to those who know me and the work we can all do, and those who just don't get it yet.

This is not a poem about revolution!

It will not scream out in protest
It will not make strong political statements
It won't make love to men with locks
It won't demand action!
It won't ask you to boycott, sign a petition or
Speak out against the government.

This is not a poem about revolution!

It will not question your conscience
It will not require intellectual critic
It won't offer solutions or change
It won't stimulate conversation
It won't uplift, inspire, motivate and it
Certainly won't promote reading, `riting, ``rithmatic, rioting
And that other taboo "R" word
Re-vo-lution.

Hell no, this is not a poem about revolution!

It will not rally on the capital steps
It will not fight for a women's right to choose
It won't be blood red
It won't be Black, African-American, or Nationalist
The only souls
That'll travel through it's veins
Will be coward soles
Running away from the frontlines
Rushing to get expensive pedicures

This is not a poem about revolution!

It will not challenge mainstream thinking
It will not get off it's ass
It won't demand Universities to develop
Black Studies Departments
Or close classes on Martin Luther King's Holiday
It will not read about African History
Cause it's an All-American poem
It will not seek Black publishers
It will not organize a rights of passage
For College graduates
It won't make you feel proud
It won't have a spiritual core
It won't demand respect
It won't have a function
It won't fly
It won't ask why?
It won't be willing to die
It won't fight the police
It won't organize
It won't make sense to everyday folk
It won't even think
About speaking Black English
It won't do a damn thing
Cause that's the kind of poetry
People like

How can you fuck without kissing?

Wax from white candles melt
Felt.
Like a romantic black and white movie
Moved me back and forth against the wall
Yanked off the matching panty and bra set
I picked up from the mall
The C-D started to stall, so we paused.
Hey y'all, sorry to interrupt.
But, how can some men avoid kissing a
woman the same time as they fuck?
Something's missing.
Confusing your brain with the organ you use to
Piss in toilets, or in dark alleys or behind dumpsters
or on woman who think it's kinky
hair tied to best posts
Stomach full from potatoes and roast
Breasts, warm like light brown toast
With wine glasses.
Examining the different shapes of women's asses
In between classes.
A sport for the masses
Of men who unconsciously rape of our dignity
Covering our mouths with tape
Throwing brown bags over our heads
Pussy without a face.
Under a kitchen, living room, or coffee house table
How are men able?
As they stride comfortably between our hips
And avoid kissing our lips
Above the neck
But not below the waist
It's okay to taste the second tongue
Ignoring the phone as it rung on our
ears their always sucking!
You don't want to hear my opinion while
we're fucking???

Wanna share your se-man?
But, not your saliva?
Too intimate to touch the tip
or lick the teeth
or bite the bottom.
All that matters is that you got him
from the back and the side
As you ride without words
Fuck what you heard!
I think it's absurd
As you ram it like a truck.
That you wouldn't want to come close
Almost
Came real.
The way true men make you feel.
But you can't deal with making her purr
You wouldn't want to kiss her with her clothes on
But you'll do her with her clothes off
Cause her skin's soft.
Lying on a rug in your loft
Just wanna get your rocks off
Just cause it was there
Not fair.
Thought you were heaven sent
Why are you afraid of being intimate?
Afraid of making love?
Cause that takes emotion
Not cherry-flavored motion-potion.
Want to suck on my tip, but not share my spit!
Love rubbing on my ass, but won't drink out my glass
of ginger beer.
It's your worst fear.
Kissing me here and there
Makes you feel like you care
For a quickie
Makes me sick
Only think with your dick
Want a trick or a hoe
Suck my toes, do you know how to go slow?
Kiss my eyelids, kiss my nose!

Don't just call out my name
Ask me my name.
Blow out the candle flame
And give me what I need
Slow, fast, wet, moist, sliding, slippery, rough
twisting, sucking.
Kiss me, yes, kiss me while we're fucking!
And I'll scream and shout
To the heavens above
Finally, I'm kissing, kissing, kissing.
Teaching you how to make love.

Womanhood Untapped

I want to give you a piece of my womanhood
You couldn't feel in my kiss
My mind can move mountains as shapely as my hips!
I'm glad you enjoy my physical peak, but if you can't stimulate my brain, then
brotha, you are weak
Seek to impress me with material things
Diamond Rings
What's happened to our Queens and Kings?
Caught up with the way one fiends for getting inside a woman's jeans, instead
of her heart and head.
I wonder if you could handle my conversation if we
weren't lying in this bed?
I'm not stuck up or saditty, but could you please raise off my . . .

And talk to me like you're a man
Sad, how you have so much to say
When you want me to stay over and over
Brother, I'm your four leaf clover
Lucky, I found you before it was too late
Using my mind as the seductive bait
Doesn't my womanhood feel good?

I knew it would.

Black Girl Juice

Maple syrup in the morning
Brown sugar that sweetens
Cinnamon twists in Apple Cider
Magic Black dust is inside her
Wheat Bread with homemade spread
This Juice goes straight to the head
Coffee without dairy cream
Any man's dream.
Black cat that'll bring you luck
Aphrodisiac you'd love to suck!
You wish! Black twisted licorice.
Cooking black- eyed- peas.
Wearing black knee-high stockings
Black pumps. black hair. black dress.
Black eyes.
This juice makes you wise
Allows the sun to shine
Black eagle. black butterfly.
Black tears she sometimes cries
But one sip and you'll believe
Braided hair natural cut or curly weave
Nails with acrylic tips, and wide-shaped hips
Most men fiend to hump her
Nails cut off she has a nice touch on her jumper.

Revolutionary waters she's your mother, auntie, sister-friend and daughter
You outta recognize her eyes
She rolls them when she's mad and she keeps her eyes wide open when she
makes love
Cause she's bad to the BONE!
Black Girl Juice is a nutritional boost
Bananas Strawberries and Melanin Nectar
No average man can affect her
Ingredients are Spicy- Mild- Sweet
Burns your tongue like an Jalepeno/ Pepper steak with authentic chopsticks

First round draft pick. Black Afro Pic.
The one with the fist!
Tight.
       Deep.
           Loose.
Have you ever tasted Black Girl Juice?
You might want to pour some inside a jar/let it linger on your top lip
Take it on a trip
Or dab small circles of it on your wrists ankles or ears
And if you're daring enough to ask...
I've got some Black Girl Juice
If you have an empty glass

Blacker The Berry

Just like the moon is only the sun cooled off
And just a touch of lotion will make tough hands soft
Some folks like it with the lights down
and others say it's scary
Still the sweetest nectar, I've found
Was in a blacker berry.
Alga syrup still covers pancakes in the hood
Never heard of Easter Bunnies or Tooth Fairies
I just hope one day I'll find a man to marry
With a blacker berry.
Deep plum. Gotta find some to boost my energy
Blackness laying on top of me
Want it to happen again
Nothing like wrapping my body around your dark skin
I know your curfews at ten
But can you stay for one more hour?
I love breathing in the scent of black flowers
Just like a hot shower's steam
I keep my eyes closed so I can remain in my black dream
Know why other women fiend
Yes, I guess I understand
The desire to want to be with a strong black man
Laying out in the sun may make your skin TAN
But, it's still not quite the same
I can't blame
You for trying
Black berry juice tears I'm crying
Boysenberry, Strawberry, Raspberry, in the cereal
Aisles can't ever find boo-berry, so Black you're blue-berry.
Not that I don't like my brothaz that are light
But have you ever made love during the day and it still feels like night?

Can I just have a itty bitty black berry bite?
Make everything society says is wrong
Feel alright

Can I just have an itty bitty black berry bite?
Make everything society says is wrong
Feel alright
Opposites might attract
But, I like my berry black
Keeps my heartbeat on track
Some folks like it with the light down
and others say it's scary.
Still the sweetest nectar I've found
Was in the blacker berry

Southern Comfort, But

He's got that southern toothpick sticking out
A set of perfect chops
And I don't ever want to ever wanna stop
Standing on my tip toes
To reach his comfortable altitude
Keep rising to the top
I kept trying to see through the clouds and thick fog
Leaving him blinded reminded me of a protest song
And I transformed many times
To be his hippy chick nationalist navigator
Stokely Carmichael inspired stewardess
Keeping it plane landing without wheels
On unlit runaways
Conductor on his freedom train
Baking revolution inside of my pre-heated oven
That still rises like a juicy lemon sun-squeezed fruit
Aiding the taste of your morning tea
You are my sunshine but cloudy days
Reappear in the whites of your eyes
Turning into tear drops wiped dry like splashes of sweat
From an afternoon of full court basketball
And your talking trash lips still look sweeter
Than the first time I felt `em against mine
Still got that silver compass you gave me
No time
Leaning your lanky limbs against my front porch pillars
Made me lose all sense of earthly direction
Your together-too cool talented twin heart toting a homemade
Zip war gun, rubberbands and a 99 cent wet and wild lipstick
Bayed at the moon danced naked every night in june and soon

You would come and sweep her off her feet
Mister black cowboy flying in on unicorn with stars and astros
Falling from your pockets

Crystal candy you would call it
Though the cinnamon-sour apple taste
Reminded me of southern cooking
The chewy texture felt more like a stale green-colored
Tangy taffy

Getting stuck in my fillings and causing toothaches without nerve
And heartaches undeserved
So I reached toward what I imagined to be an endless blue sky
To grab the toothpick from your lips
And suddenly, I slipped
Realizing only angels really fly
And you ain't up that high
Why I never thought your blackness becoming my outer-space
Inside, was just a tiny place
Where pigtails turn to porn queens
And making love on moonbeams
Was just a SCI-fi freak dream team
You were my Olympic gold-colored carrying cusswords and Louisiana Hot
sauce on the tip of my tongue
A licky-hot kiss pressed against your 501's or nine to five's
Cause you couldn't work no real job
You were busy basking your brown skin in baptized bottles
Of raindrops
As I worked to quench your thirst by any means of necessary
Instead of deep inside to sea me diving
Arriving to the surface out of breath
I counted on your oxygen
Not hot air balloons rides along your sexy lower lip
Gypped I climbed off the bionic man I created
Inflated

I go along for my last ride
Nose dive head first
Get off my slip and slide
Cause change gone come when hunger pains
For your yahoo and yum yum
Gonna get beat down by hollow heart drums
Tree bark sticks
And those love-hate *Do The Right Thing* fists
That'll steal away a southern toothpick
Sticking out a set of perfect chops
And I don't ever wanna stop

Clark and Indigo

Dedicated to the vision of Spike Lee and all women of color searching for the prescription to feel mo' betta.

You said you wanted green leaves
Natural locks
Concrete creeks kissing
Moon lit parks
So, why you still doing Clark?
I grew out my perm
Goodbye lye
After lie
You said you wanted to tie
Me up with Kente
One day move to Ghana
Ria isn't as bad as irritating
As your mental disease
You're growing your locks so long
But your mind has lost its keys
Still wet behind the ears
From the waters in Clarks sauna
How was I supposed to know?
I thought you wanted Indigo
We're a revolutionary team
Dreams dipped in afro sheen
Keen to our third eye
Cooking sweet potato pies
When you really love America's
Juicy red apples
Snapples just Kool-aid
In a glass
Our conversations rooted in our past
You said you love my lips singing liberation lyrics
And all that booty shaking music
You never wanted me to hear it
On the frontlines
Of hypocritical hype
I thought a deep down sista
Was your type
Oh, how you used to boast

Bout moving to the Ivory Coast
Full of hope
I didn't know you
We're talking about Ivory
Soap on a rope
Damn
So here I am giving up ham
Health Conscious
And heart beating
To ancestral drums
Teaching our children
Where we're from
Black bees hum
As you come creeping
While I'm sleeping
Eyes never close
I'm your sun, your moon,
Your queen!
But at night you want your hoes?
Suppose I styled my hair
Relaxed it straight to my face
Threw on a fly mini skirt
And put make up over my natural race
Sport some sexy lingerie
Play games with your mind
Manipulate your mental
So, you can be
Just like me
Another schizophrenic
Down sista
Who don't know who
You want her to be
Free your weave
And conscious men will follow
So, you assume my straight hair
Means my heart is hollow
Swallow pills to keep me thin
So, I'll fit in to corporate clothes
You've ironed to my skin
After sex trophy

For your arm
My smiles got so much charm
When I'm not talking
You want a woman from
Substance
Abuse
Loose and loving
Bouncing Black Barbie
Got a gift Garvey
And something for you too.
A prescription for all fly
Hat to the back
High heel wearing
Conscious cutie
Braid Blow-drying
Gold tooth sportin'
B-girl walking
Evening gown gripping
Poland Springs drinking
Gold Hoop ear ring wearing
Singing Coltrane to
A Tribe Called Quest track
Mac Divas
Doing dirt with angels grin
Full - figured
Neatly trimmed
Penny Loafers
Brown leather "Tims"
Tied
In Red Ribbon
Halle Berry or Robin Givens
Living life in two
I'm all these things
I thought you knew
Melanin medicine
Can cure the flew
And now that I'm over you

I'm Mo' betta
I'm Mo' betta
Indigo-Clark honey dipped sista
Black
Without all the blues

Black Statue Of Liberty

I stand still above an Island, fists straight in the air
Scar on my face, thick braids in my hair.
Battle boots tied, red blood in the tears I've cried
Tourists fly from all over just to swim near my tide
Or climb up my long flight of stairs.
But they trip on their shoe string lies.
Piece by Piece they shipped my body to this country
Now that I'm here, your people don't want me
I'm a symbol of freedom, but I'm still not free
I suffer from class, race and gender in-equality
I wear a crown of knowledge, cause I'm a conscious queen
My mask is one of happiness, though my history here is full of misery.
Done Deliberately.
I am America's true statue of liberty.
You placed a bible under my arm, after you ripped me of my faith
And made me pray to a fictionary impostor
So, if you were trying to maintain liberty
Too late, you just lost her
Cause her torch is about to serve as the night light for truth
In the slums and the ghettos that you find so uncouth.
Education will be delivered not from the tree, but the root.
So, little black girls and boys will check their pockets for spirituality Rather
than loot.
Cause liberty is just old mother nature
And although you don't love her, she'll never hate ya.
She's earth, wind and fire, don't tempt her to show her power.
Turning all weeds to flowers.
Looking into her wise eyes will make a blind man see
How can you dare name an eurocentric girl after me?
Assata Shakur Barbara Jordan Nikki Giovanni and Angela Davis.
These are the real symbols of liberty, cause that stone faced French Woman
ain't gonna save us.
The same folks who enslaved us.

I'm sitting at the back of the bus, cause I feel like it.
And I play ball

Not cause you pay me to dunk it, dribble it or hike it.
I'm taking all my people back home, and breaking them mentally free.
I am the walking, talking, breathing, beautiful statue of liberty.
I sweep crack pipes out school yards
I nurture my man when times are hard.
So, where the hell's my statue?
What's a liberated woman gotta do?
Place my name in wet cement
Every month I pay the rent.
Put my silhouette on a stamp
I'm not a ho, slut or tramp.
My children aren't on crack, and either am I
I want to see the words, " Go strong Black woman," when the good year
blimp flies by.
I can bake cookies, bare babies, reside over revolutions, get rings out of tubs,
wear a suit, sport baggy jeans, slick my hair back,
Or tie it back in braids.
My aura is unafraid.
So, no statue in the big apple can mess with me.
I am the walking, talking, surviving, breathing, beautiful ,
Black statue of liberty.

What really happens

This is the twilight zone
Full color one a.m. New York time
Three a.m. in Detroit
I am an Apollo legend
But I'm not old or dead yet
Strangers got pieces of my braid extensions
In their pockets
I took my hair down on Monday
Tree knew in Jersey by Wednesday
Crest asks me to smile for them

Free!!

Free to be me

It's showtime and my teeth are falling out
Cause I can't afford the dentist
A popular artist's only kind of life insurance
Everyone will think you're big time
Your rent will still be kicking your ass
Past the prententious literary elitist
Who freed their self hate with Suburban
Dipped salad forks
When I'm just trying to eat a warm bowl of Alphabet Soup
Poets always say,
"I don't think poets should compete."
Self-claimed vegetarian eating meat
When no one's looking
Just cause no one understands you
Doesn't mean that you're deep
And I'm telling you.....!!!! (singing like vesta)
I guess I'm not a poet
I just play one on TV
I ain't a poet cause poets spend too much time
Masturbating metaphors
When I just want casual sex
By myself
Ball - pointed felt - tipped

Cafe equipped With coffee beans
Latte' illuminate lovers

Discover Detroit Red ain't dead
I'll rip the Cowrie shells out your head
Instead of imagining what it must
Be like to really live the words
This is MY LIFE
My 3-for-a-dollar kidney beans
Brown rice, marinara, spaghetti
And sweet plantain

When have you offered personality
Alamode With your poem?
Pulsating my heart's still waiting
To feel you
Breathe out brilliance
Bootlegs of bougee bar-b-que sentence
Since our integrity is at *steak*
Where's the beef?
Thief of commas curse words and common sense
Less unorganized wise wordsmiths
Kiss my scars/Poetic superstar
Buy me back my car!
Send my remains back to Mars
If you don't love my scorpion brown eyes
Keep my name off your flyer
Poetry pulls fistfuls of New York Borough boundaries

Drowning the beauty
Watering down realities

Poetry ain't about you or me
College tours or getting in free
Blowing up the spot or impressing poets
We see smell and taste all the time
It's about baby girl Black statue of Liberties
Reading the same words at family reunions
Pursuing poetry with Number 2 pencils on Black page
And if I don't move you

Then my poem wasn't for you anyway!
And if my metaphors don't
mesmorize the prolific
Terrific
Cause I'm still gonna fuse
femininity fearlessly
Dipped in baggy blues
While you dazzle Cafe revolutionaries
Always claiming the keep it Black
But never willing to give it back

So, If you have issues
Cause my work can be loved inside the
Starving bellies of the everday mass

Kiss my poetic athletic everday . . .

Beautiful

Beautiful
To me
You must be
Bathing in ivory soap
Steady trying to cope
With the fact that my skin's black
So's yours
But still, you don't like how I feel
Blond-hair pert shampoo commercial overkill
Three meals a day
No more beautiful black men come out to play
Not even on beautiful black nights
My skin's not white
Not on the front page.
Unless the article's on black rage!
So, why are you suprised?
Blue eyes, haunting our blue skies
On TV guides
And you don't know why
So many Black people abandon their own
Too many black women home alone
So, hopefully some black insight's shone
Into your goldilocks, as the fake reality clock
Keeps ticking —ticking
Only see black faces on advertisements for
Chicken —Chicken
So, I think it's my duty
To make you recognize my beauty
Like little white lies
Diamonds ain't really a rarity
Revolution parody
Queen coming with conscious clarity
Of why my brothas dare to be
Trying not to Marry me!
Beautiful I must be
As you lie in the sun
My people die with loaded guns
in their mouths

Suicide is genocide
Still on this mythical beauty tip you ride
Pale face Lipstick Red Ruby
And Nile nNefertiti Nubian
Not knowing why our brothas
Confusing caucasian with quality
Of black beauty in the mirror he
Can't help but see me
Beauty goes past skin
But not kin
When will children freely swing in the park?
Dark scars, moles and tattoos
Are beauty marks
Miss Clairol don't know it all
Holding my brothas up
So they don't fall into foreign hands
From foreign lands Can't understand.
Why you don't understand
How it's out of place
For you to criticize our race
Cause our culture was wiped out
Without a trace of a tear from your face
Fire hoses and sprays of mace
Laced up in a legacy of lap top computers
To this country we aren't commuters.
So, I hope one day you'll distinguish
Between Black English
And the talk we've learned to talk
And the God we've learned to pray to.
And the skin we've learned to hate
Surgically removing our African traits
Bleaching our skin with Clorox
Unorthodox
To not recognize the reason
Treason.
During a war when people of color
Fighting to find who they are
Care more about cars
While the government kills quotas
I question your motives

So, I will with revolution
Razor cuts
Slash society's sick symbol of so-called beauty
Cosmopolitan Cutie
Wearing cranberry taffeta
Can't compare to the fabric of Africa
Can't help but laugh at ya.
Wanting to be my brotha's lover
And he's doing you undercover
Pretending like it will last
But first he must know his past
And you must realize
Why thousands of black women cry
While their babies sit on the knee of
Santa's claws
Wishing they were white because
They get all the good toys

That's the makings of a confused black
Boy or girl.
It's this confused messed up world.
You don't have something better.
America has folks' brains on a tether.
Whether the weather is rainy
My brotha still beautiful to me
Whether the snow is freezing

Whether the weather is rainy my brothas are still
Beautiful to me

And Whether the snow is freezing
In him, I still believe
And if you really want to shelter black men
From the storm.
Just acknowledge the black women who
For centuries kept them warm
Cause only someone with knowledge is suitable
Nothing confusing about a black man finding himself in the
Reflection of a black woman.
It's simply beautiful.

Genocide

Disappearing down dangerous downgrades don't dread die down in dungeons doped up dummies deliver delight devilish deeds done

Damon. Darnell. Derrick. Derron. Dez and Dennis Died.
From Genocide.

Jump higher when the bullets are shot at your feet.

Just pray to this God and chew on this meat.

Jonathan. James. Juwan. Joe and Jack.
Are all in jail for life just because they're Black.

Hurry hope to hoop.   Hanging in Hell Have to Hide.
From Genocide.

Politicians putting pate' on pizza push proposals pretending punks paying prices proving our people without power perping plastic pansies

All for a plate to place a piece of apple pie.
Paul Pascal Paris and Pete just died.

Schizophrenic stereotypical stationary steps stop secretly saying sorry so someday slaves stand. Still stinking sails on salty seas save stones/smoke/seriously/sane stories sabotaging silence saint somebody stole sound and sight from
Samon. Sadeek. Stan. Steven and Sam.
Damn. Another one of my brotha's got that disease and died.

Gotta find a cure for genocide.

The Words don't FIT in my mouth

Chase it down with spring water
Poison choking boys and girls
Twirls young tongues in knots
Forgot how to pronounce
Gargling with malted ounce
Punk   you wait!
Punk   you wait for them
Punk   you wait in Old English
Distinguished
Punk u wait for them
Punk u wait for them
Punkuwaitforthem Punkuwaitforthem
PunkuwaitforthemPunkuwaitforthem
Punkuwait Punkuwait Punkuwait
Puncuate Puncuate
Period.
Dem dialects don't work
Words don't fit like sexy slave skirts
Hurt inside language died
On salty shores down south
Words don't fit right in my mouth
Can't be ART!
Split apart full lips injected with sexy puffy lies
Tries to kiss Africa with French
Vous-allez avec moi, Ce Soir?
Uncomfortable twists   causing lisps
Low attention spans
All retalin reading is banned
As traditional chants are turned into
Cheeleader rants
Mumbled memories of what mouths used to do
Threw away like old souls of shoes
Our feet never wanted to really wear

Dare to bite down with borrowed bone teeth
Chew away the discomboulated food lies
And still teach   .
Gargling with small G's you worship

Vomiting up violent vowels
A-E-I-O-U
nothing
For unfeeling oragel mouth
Chewing away at our gums
Drugged and X-rayed some days
We feel the thrill as you drill into caves and cavities
Still can't find black poet correctly defined in
Nary Chun Dics
Dic tion narys
But there's blown up illustrations
Of Tom Dick and Harry
Scary letters fell from Alphabet
Bid Buy Black Bodies
Somebody sold the sun
So begun birth of darkness
And the majesty of moonlight
Shining light on melanin mommas
Forming fallopian tubas
Blowing babies breath
Stretched canal mouth
Pushing out Black piano keys
Playing with blind Ray eyes
First cries sing as slave children swing
From umbilical cords
Choking vaginal vocals

She's unable to scream
So she holds in her pain
Pushing out new life
Naming her music woman bass
Traced to the taste of Lawry's spice
Black eyed peas and brown rice
Incites riots
Rubs out the red better than visine
She's a shapely silouhette against
Salty shores down south

Words don't fit right in my mouth

So we twist your nigga nouns
Assault adjectives Violent verbs
Heard the function function
Of conjuctons could kill
When connecting a poet with a pen
When you rip out our hearts with
Required eight parts of speech
Poets like Sharrif, Brad, Carmen, Saul, Tony Medina,
Aurora, Asha, Mums, Brown and Shakey connect
Like original continents
Continuing to teach
Amazed?
We are prepositional phrase
In your face
Around your block
That good stock
Escaping brain damaging drugs
Bopping our heads to the lies in
School house rock

No longer nervous to have the nerve to be us
Bused into integration experiments
Our language changes transcends
Turning black to pink
By switching the color of our ink
Ubators giving re-birth to a poetic sound
That's always been around
Now its cool to be down
don't be afraid of the poets of the Hip Hop generation
Internationally invading your intellectual institutions
past present and future tense sense
When did we start licking the bottoms of labels that rename us

The renaissance reborn

Our words never digested like corn
I'd like to buy a vowel or at least recommend a poet
To spin the damn wheel
Cause we've always been writing as our tortured tongues
Bleed from biting down on nine to five words

That don't fit
I'd rather spit than speak
Curse out commas
The correct way to say mother

Can't be momma
Notes home read
quote
"My teacher can't understand what I wrote"
Cause I spoke without waiting for the punks
End quote
Punk u wait without a fuss
In this language there is no trust
Where as/ There of/ There for

Poetry will remain universal language
Without clout
Bout to sprinkle antoynms and cinnamon
On brown french toast
Boast when we find creative ways to fix and fit
Poison cherry-flavored popsicle stick shaped
Words in our mouths
Melting into metaphors
Mutating into talkative tongue-tied tourists
Mumbling about ivory coast memories

That remain unfound
And if they still don't understand what
We're talking about
Tell them their words don't fit in our mouths
Exclamation point
!
Period
.

My caged bird don't sing, and. every Black bird ain't a piece of fried chicken

To the beauty of Alicia (a.k.a. Blue), Nicole Gilbert, Marnell, Alexis and all divas that grace the world with their spirit through songs no one can ever steal away.

My caged bird don't sing
It cries
Stolen wings can't fly
Cause they took away our music
My caged bird don't sing
It cries
Stolen wings can't fly
Cause they took away our music
Makers
Soul takers
Turning trees to twigs
Fed us worms from pigs
Robbed our nests
At best
Baby Birds
Learn how to fly
Across foreign skies
Make it across
Lost
Millions on that ship
With settlers looking like Gilligan
Figuring out ways to steal again
Anotha loafa Sankofa
Word
African Bird
Never heard a flock Still in shock
Carrying Glocks
We are the tock of the clock
But we forgot
Planet rocket to the planet rock
Don't stop
Don't pass go
Straight to hell
Bird dressed in blue

Locked in a red pod zoo
And all the walls were white
Typical African bird plight
Tight as it seems
Bird had those genes
To sing Negro spirituals
Dropping base off his beak
Bellowing beats quite lyrical
Performing miracles
Magnificent enough to rebuild
The walls of Jericho
Here we go Here we go
Here we go Here we go
Here we Here we Here we go
DMC and DJ RUN
My caged bird don't sing
Cause they took away her drum
Beat
Clawed feet
Leaving droppings on cross burners
Wearing sheets
Shackled together
Black tar babies covered in feathers
Wearing America's old past time tether
Didn't make that caged bird sing a thing
But the whole village knew she could play the harmonica
With her heart flute
Breathe life into lungs
Make babies come
Still, that caged bird didn't sing a peep
Cause she saw her family moved out like sheep
And she recognized the wolves shooting at her feet
Find a way to get a grip
Might fly off this slave ship
Or take the pain of another ass kicking
See, every Black bird ain't a piece of fried chicken
And every heart beat
I mean drum beat
Heart beat
Drum beat

Heart beat
Drum beat
Heart Drum Heart Drum
Heart Heart Drum Drum
DRRRUUMMM
Beat
Ain't for sample
Or sale
Well?
Are you men?
Wait
Are you birds or mice?
Vanilla Ice ice baby
Caged birds don't sing
They cry
Stolen wings can't fly
Cause they took
Away our music
My caged bird don't sing
It cries
Stolen Wings can't fly
Cause they took away our   music

Colorstruck!

*excerpt from my play, The Revolutions in the Ladies Room... Performed at The Nuyorican Poets Cafe in 1996.

Hey Baby, can I have your phone number?
I really prefer your light skin
That's what he told me quite boldly
The whole thing was scary
He didn't think I'd relate to the
Blacker the Berry
He's skin was like mine
I guess he wanted us to bond
Like a weaves hair glue
Fool
I started to talking to the brotha in Haiku
He still didn't understand
Putting down my sistas was not the way
To win my hand
Me down mentality
Brotha so white-washed
He couldn't see his own dirty laundry
And he didn't want to come clean
So, I started taking him to school
I said, don't be ashamed cause Melanin is cool
Still, he insisted on enlightening me
Frightening me
I was out of luck
Light-skinned brotha was color struck
Run-a-muck
Silly punk
Wanted to place my sistas face
Next to a brown paper bag
Now, Isn't that the job of the so-called" man"
Brown, Copper, Coal, Sand or Tan
We should all be the same to you
Black
Man.

Gotta understand why my darker sistas are mad
Now you think she's pretty cause Afro-centric
Is your fad
Kente Cloth and Cowry shells
Oh, unconscious brotha you wear it well
Around your neck, hangs a gold cow bell
That rings out the words
"House nigga for sale."
No, I don't want your number!

Stretch this message
Across America's
New found interest in
Multi-culturism
Mixed with hidden agendas
When the
Alterior motive
Is to kill more quotas
Someone lied
Cause we've always
had Apartheid
It's existed for years
Bi Tri or Multi
Cultural folks didn't just
get here
Fresh off the boat
Finding a way to stay afloat
Despite the lies in laws they wrote
To vote
For yet another category for
minority
Another reason for ignoring me.
Some pretty eyed passing boys and girls
like the game.
Shame.
Curly doo's that hate locks
Only listening to rock
And rolls like a dog when the
master cracks his whip
Sipping on imported anything.
Heard you like to tap and sing
So, You're a futuristic house negro
Dropping micro-chips in
your own people's afros.
Ashamed to choose a
dark-skinned lover
You're mommas white
So, you're an Other!
Peel off the panelin

Box This!

check in your
senses here

Cause I recognize the melanin
In your skin
Don't have to ask where you've been
If you're from Jamaica
They'll still hate ya
Puerto Rican - Black
Speaking Spanish
Wanna ban us
When we need to unite
But with our own heritage
We fight
Cause we're ashamed.
You're half French, One-fourth Indian, Portuguese,
White, Mexican, and your great grandmama's
from Brazil
Still
You insist.
Mr. and Mrs. Mixed
None of your ancestors
ever been enslaved
But your skin be darker than me
So, who you be?
Brotha and Sistas with Locks and Braids
Silky Hair straight when not relaxed
Trying to get your blackness back
By checking the next available category
Multi-Cultural surgery
No government box
Can label me
Check the box next to queen
Mother of all nations
Staying black like the Haitians
Did we forget about the Moors
Let's give Egyptians, Ethiopians and Ecuadorians
their own box
And white folks who let their thin hair lock
It's no suprise
Too many people of color on the rise
Not afraid of the sunshine
Or shades of gray

We're still the majority

You're tactics are boring me.
But my people
We still be soaring see.
Using the word diversity
To Separate those with mixed ancestry
The Beatles sing let it be
Let's just wipe it out!
Colored in South Africa
Or North America
Won't bring you any clout
Too many have already died
From Apartheid.
Shame.
If we allow them to use
Multi Cultural Music
Don't Confuse it
With something new
Cause those same drum beats
Originated in Africa too.
It's senseless
The whole US Census
Since this
Country created race
To justify slavery
Stop beleaguering
The point.
Ancestors anoint
The mentally dead
And above water from
firehoses
Help us tread.
It's a step BACK.
It's okay to say you're black
Even if you're light brown.
Cause we're all earthy ground
Yellow Sun, Black Berries Lightly Toasted
Alabama Red-Bone Clay
Honey Roasted from the Ivory Coast

Along the Hudson River
In the depths of the Nile
You're in Denial
America's a multi-cultural

Indian-Giver
Indian Killer
Still gonna call you a multi-cultural
Nigger
So I figure
Leave people of color
without a name
Keep your shame shock
Therapy
Being Multi-Cultural
Won't make you free
Realize
Even blond hair and green eyes
Burst through the same canal
Grew inside the same womb
Of Africa's mother earth
Sucked on the same black breast
Manifest a category for that.
A black leopard with white spots
Ain't a new breed of cat
A wild animal hard to tame.
Africans in America
Scrub off the shame.

Sesame Street

*Can you tell me how to get
How to get to Sesame Street
How to get to Sesame Street*

Suuunny days melted like yellow crayon
Against hot ovens heating up winter get-a-way
Houses
In the hood
Lums hide in stylish hairdo's
Wrapped in Moshood
Cowrie shells courtesy of Anne Klein
Iron-pressed behinds
Switch in off-beat rhythms
On runways some still call streets
Neat nails snap
Pedicured toes tap
At all the right times

Who are the people in your neighborhood?
It's the other people that you meet
When there's no Black business on your street
There's just not enough of us
Showing up late like Snufulufugus
Cappuccino forming crust
On phony top lips
Drip between smiiling

Gaps in communication
Temptation to turn nose up
To sky
Sophisticated Black angels
Praying for anti-ghetto wings
One of these doesn't belong here
One of these things is not quite the same
Can you tell me who the hell we be here?
Fear of friendly fire
From hard cores
Sporting fronts

Don't take the "A" Train after eight
Wait
Excuse me, Black intellectual elite

Can you tell me how to get to Sesame Street?

Afraid to move east
Wearing skin whole wheat
Acting like you never ate
Peanut butta and jelly
Or bumped and grinded
To R-Kelly
On the living room couch
Your girl or boy
Oscar the grouch
On the lookout
Here comes anotha hand-crafted

Kente cloth cutie
Carrying a coach bag
Hiding the tag
On the inside
Of a pyramids stomach
Grows a project kid
Did you forget how to be broke
It's been so long
Got mony green flowing
Like kermit the frog
Conscious brotha

Big chicken yellow colored bird
Bouncing BMW's
Parked on slopes
Living in Fort Green
Sherwood Forest
Housing in Queens
Do you see what I see
We lost souls
Roll eyes
I mean politely bat

Walk our leashed cats
Camellions camouflaging
Dogging Hip Hop heads
When they really want to be down
With MC's smoking trees
I hug

In the hood
If you knew what I knew
You would too
Mister and Misses
Nutri-sweet
Inviting over
Electric
Politically correct company
Can you tell me
How to get a reality bite
From a pit
Bull
Sick of all the bullshit
Left on the bottom of
African feet

Can you tell me
How to get out
How to get out
Of Sesame Street?

Anticipation

The crowd is loud, people talking about yesterday and such
I don't mind that much.
I'm silent
watching mouths moving, saying something,
but I can't hear
cause you aren't here
Guess yesterday means nothing
If your spirits gone tomorrow

Silence is my haven, inside my mind, I hear your voice.

Quiet still, I look to heaven,
Trying to feel you in my world
But it's not working, where's your voice?
I heard your call, I want to answer,
but now it's so unclear
I'm searching for some shelter, get my heart outta fear

Wish you would just walk into my life, the crowd just keeps on
walking, talking as I sit.
A painful way to hear you now
blending with the rest of sound,
just one moment to myself, is all I ask,
is that too much?
The crowd still loud,
people talking about yesterday and such,
and here I am just sitting, waiting,

longing for your touch.

Can you hear me?!

I'm in love with potential

I keep falling in love with potential
But it never seems to work out
He was full of a lot of it
And he was TALL
But potential had a way of becoming diluted with insecurities
And just cause you can see the beauty of someone
Doesn't mean they can see it for themselves
Still I believed potential would eventually love me as much I loved him
Then begin to love himself the way I loved myself
But there was someone else
There always is
Potential had an influential way of showing me what my potential was
And he celebrated all I could do without him
Potential reminded me of how he loved my commitment to doing whatever I
had to do to exercise my own potential
Even if that meant potentially leaving him behind

Still I unconditionally loved potential and held on to the potential future we
could have if only he would see our potential without being intimidated by
my own potential

If he would just stop loving me with conditions

Especially when I loved him simply for the possibility of how great he could
become and already was but didn't know it cause he was caught up in my
potential, instead of seeing my life as a reflection of what he already had or
what we could potentially have together

And that meant loving you when you hadn't yet reached your full potential
But helping you get there as quickly as possible
Isn't it just a bit too easy to fall in love with someone after the glory and not
along the slow, goal setting, potential way?

And if I didn't love your possibilites then I didn't love you
And if you didn't realize our possibilities because you were too wound up in
my potential
then you didn't really love me

I guess sometimes we give potential too much credit
And borrow interest from our own accounts
without taking ourselves into account
How many times did I blow off your behavior relying on potential?
I can no longer count
Or wait around for you to let me stand naked in front of you
So you can see yourself as worthy of my love

You loving me for me and not through me

Can really be potentially dangerous

Yellow people are brown on the tips

For Pierre
A female banker loves a guy who works in a shoe store,
because he is a poet too.

The sun rises even when it's cold
I've got orange sunflowers growing out my palms
The spit from your summer kisses keeps my stem wet
Reddens the pink of my lips

You told me, Yellow people are Brown on the tips

Have you ever felt the equator around your waist
after a movie?
Or fallen in love with the perfect taste of pineapple
on a slice of pizza?
This is a love story about the secret daughter of the mau mau
And the ressurection of our children
Maybe it's just about the dreams people in love share

A tide on the seaport watches the urgency of your love for me
Rushing to swim among the play toys in the tub
Our daughter waits on the shore of yesterdays couldabeen afterbirth
She builds castles of seven shells and climbs to the top smoking oxygen
through a plastic staw
Her lungs are looking for familiar air and she doesn't care
who's watching her greenhouse affected eyes
raining water
She places several soft baby kisses on a silver ring
Throws it into the ocean for her daddy to find
Drained and dull without diamonds
It is the symbol of our meeting twice
In a lifetime
And the life that's yet to come

Concealed in the incubator of imagination, tears and tomorrows
You see my full round belly in perfect color
We practice the pushing and breathing techniques
While making love
We realize someday we're gonna have to let the seed return

To her original position inside of me
Our mouths sweat the letters of her name
All over our bodies
She is chosing us now
We wipe away our future with polyester towels
Still warm from the dryer
I ask you what making loves means
If we always end up throwing away what we make
Cleaning up our spilled mistake

You painted pictures of me in a long fitted wrap skirt by a window
Flaming orange hair against the clouds
Your hands are shaking
There is no frame to fit the striking resemblence

No blame for lonely Decembers

The expressway was salted
As our families drove past one another
In the rear glass of my daddy's convertible white cadillac
I drew our names in melted frost
with my little girl fingers
You wave and tell me to meet you in sands box
So I came

Didn't recognize you with your hair locked

Still there was an incredible view that our hands quickly knew
So we clicked seven times without shoes
You were afraid to touch me with the blue pale you carried with two hands
It was filled with swirling dirt and silver water
You eventually reached in and I felt your fingertips gently braile the lining of
my embryonic sac
You wiped mud from the ring sitting at the bottom
Against soft brown skin
Circles of water washed right below my navel
Mixing with the fertility of fresh fish
The smell takes over in the morning and you tell me stories
Of all the bodies thrown off the edge of the port
We were ready for the rescue of one little girl

Drowning in confusion, colors
And clocks that told us we were too young
To have babies back then
You put the ring on my second to last finger
Mother my need to finally let go of the child
Growing inside for seven hundred years
You tell me you love me when I sleep
But their is a simple beauty of waking up with water blue
breath choking at childhood's ankles unshakled
She sings the songs we once taught her
In a snow dessert storm she learns to walk
Our connection surrenders to the truth thirsty from the
lost words of tongue
She is our first born daughter
In the honey dew of daybreak
We marry
And the wind calls her name in celebration
Assata!

Poetry is my man

Poetry pays my rent better than Babyface
poetry takes his hands, gently touches every raised part of my face
massages my temples my poetry is confident and caring
smart enough to sometimes be simple
Poetry plays conscious lyrics
Blows bass through brass
poetry braids my hair
ties it to his armchair-revolutionaries beware
poetry walks me home late at night
holds my hands supplies me with a shoulder to cry on
and on and on
my poetry is sometimes long never short as a haiku
why you smiling?
you know my poetry too?
He's got a little southern twang all through the night
he likes to hang   his coat in my closet
or kick it in my back pack
he sits with me on train rides inspires
kisses my body from head to toe when I'm tired
my poetry is black caramel cocoa khaki never lacks the
Sensitivity to satisfy if he can
Poetry throws rocks at my windows teaches me the crescendo

Poetry is my man

my poetry never lies to me
cause real poetry is simply truth
poetry doesn't send me flowers but always provides the root
my baby, poetry, can break down political prison sentences
into short paragraphs
conjugate verbs through spoken words
and yes, poetry even makes me laugh
My poetry always comes home to me at night
adjusts my pillows
he brings the ooh ah oh and oomm he combs
caresses undresses
my poetry's got game for days
beatboxes heart-shaped halos over his head

wears smooth bald heads neat fades and long dreads
likes the way I chew my pen tops
holds together my HIPS
so we can create jazzclassicsoldiesbutgoodiesr&brock and roll
newwavehousetechno - slow it down add his base
Slooowwlly create the HOP
my poetry is a warrior holding black smoke in his lungs
he exhales speaking in multiple tongues
my poetry is bionic more mind-blowing then cypress chronic
created ebonics always been hooked on phonics
my poetry is a strategist yet sporadic
likes to make love to my canvas
not just wait till the middle of the night so he can
TAG IT
poetry kills me softly with his song
I'm his best friend instead of his dog
poetry takes over my notebook
street knowledge college book stealing crook
stimulating my black stylo unleashing
African-Colored-American-Negro-Okay, well Black
muscular melanin drops of ink
my poetry's shit don't stink
He is required reading

L O V E   P O E M

If casual "what ups"
Meant I love you
Then you must be love sick

If not hearing the sound of my raspy voice
In your ear
Or my breath no larger warming your neck
Made you want me
You must be fiending

If telling my close friends you knew I was really
Your soul mate counted
Then time is over
The clock has stopped
And somewhere we must be together

If not seeing me made you miss my face
Or wonder If I missed you too
Then my heart is a.w.o.l.
Walking in circles
Searching without eyes
Trying to see you
Living and breathing
Without me
Returning to my body
After seven attempts/without a trace
Faced with the reality/I've lost my reflection

If making love to me when I asked you to
Meant you wanted to be with me forever
Then I am pregnant with your SUN We live on the moon!
And now you can finally

See the

Light

If every time you crossed my mind our thoughts were
linked
Then we must be conversing all night long and hours are too short
Cause you want to feel every minute of my life inside me

But

That's not you

If every time you made music/ My teardrops were your sweat
And those base-lined beats and kicks were your love song
Then we are swimming in a Hip Hop LL- Cool - Jay "I need love" hook

If the longer we were away from one another
Our love grew stronger
Than my heart muscles can move mountains and pounce on past lovers
Who test you

If you heard me everytime I told I loved you
When you weren't around
Then you already know the ending to my fairy tales
And you've rescued me many times from the nightmarish thought
That it's not you
On the horse
Below my window
In my life

If every time you took a walk
You followed my footsteps
Then you must know I'm on my way over
Coming and calling just because
I was who I was
And that was part of you

If uncertain good-byes meant you didn't need to bother with hellos
Temporary weekends were only practice
For honeymoons and romantic summer vacation spots
Then you'd be here
But
You're not.

peeling away
at my tempting
surface
twisting my mind like
a long brown stem
cutting me in half,
saving pieces of me in
the fridge for when
you're hungry a little
later.
I'm a popular fruit, but
you can have your
pick.
you peel. you bite. you
lick.
fulfill all my
needs

APPLE SEED

tenderly you
eat me up
I plant my apple seed
wonder if you'll have
a craving once again
a sugar substitution
for a healthy freak
maybe next week
you'll pull me out of
that cold square box
apple juice on the
rocks
I love it when you
take the lead
searching for my
apple seed.

Five Percent of Maine or Don't Mess With Motha Nature

You are fall leaves
Painted orange and bright yellow
In October
Brown bark twisted like pretzel
Up tall trees
Making love to earth every day
Delicious and dirty
Bumble Bees, fear your sting
Tracy Chapmans "mountain of things"
Move here to make simple
Dreams come true
Mysterious honey dew
Sticky-fingered you
Wash your body along
Silent shores
Warm winds take homage
On your smooth dark back
As invisible children
Carrying water barrels
On their head
Swing on playsets they've
Created from your shoulder-bone clay
Rock hard, yet soft
Enough to feed millions
Of growing seeds
You cultivate culture
Naturally
Nurture a nation
Without fee
Urban representative
Rural Royalty
River Free
Clouds capture your head
For Pillow
Willow Trees
Whisper secrets
When you walk

You bad, motha
Natives know you can deliver drought
Big city bad girl
Got old-fashioned girl clout
Massage her tired neck
She's at home
Trace the veins along her hands
She is motha nature
And you're walking
On Her stolen land
Mistaken for a foreigner
Amazed by stars at night
But momma's pregnant womb
Water breaks
Reflects the sun
Setting off electric lightening
Strike.
Don't be afraid of her
Thick-locked roots
Speaking to sparrow
Connecting with crows
Somehow she just knows
Communicating without tongue
The crack of dawn is her
daughter
Slaughtered Native people
Her brother, father and sun
Round hills
Sculptured Hips
Men have climbed
And even sipped
Ripped her soil
With crack and whip
Shut lipped and legs tied
Skies cried
As she screamed
Moon beams melted
Earth opened up it's seams
Swallowing almost everything
But you could still hear feminine laughter

From Motha Nature's rapture
Echoing songs from children jumping rope
Minus shoes
Riding bare back horses
Galloping ghosts
Without clue
For many it was so hard to believe
Watching sexy seasonal tease
As she quickly gathered up her things
Continuing her long October journey
Changing the color of green fall leaves.
You bad, motha.
You bad.

Mo'dusa

Off with her head
Off with her head
That's what they said

Turning men to stone
Tone dark dread
Said her African hips
Ripped through the myths
Of Greek-ology
Without apology
African Arrogance
Stared you in your face
Godly grace
Sending shock waves
Through electric outlets
Plugged into moonlight
Little Ben Franklin's kite
Caught in the color or Black sky
Wonder why
Darkness makes the room so bright
The moon's got melanin adrenaline rush
They huffed and puffed
Trying to turn brown eyes blue
Black man producer
Silent seducer
Most can stand African Modusa
Makes most wanna holler
Off with her head
Off with her head
That's what they said
Snakes
Mistaken for poison
Ask my boys and
They'll tell you it's all a myth
Minus happiness
Wanna run their hands through hair
That's the nappiest

Nefertitti free thee
Face
Won't eliminate
The race
Womb still working
Birthing
Miracle makers
Minimized by your lust
Mind high from angel dust
If she must Modusa still flies with
Clipped wings
Dust daughters ain't afraid of no dirt
Her work stopped wars
Beauty untouched
Men opened doors
In the middle of fightin'
Who lied when they were writing
Clash of the Titans
Biting Modusa's style
Her funky braids
Attitudinal switch
Lynched
Which of you allowed her to be dead?
Looked away when they screamed
Off with her head
Off with her head
That's what they said

Where were the sista savers?
Salivating at the mouth
As she spoke with neck broke
Dangling from dem oak trees
Modusa's mirror image
Brought all men to their knees
In prayer
How dare we make ourselves
scared
To claim conscious cutie
Carved from soul clap clay
Have we forgotten

Picking cotton
Wasn't the only time
We sang songs from spiritual hums
Heard only when modusa
Hung her head high
Creating Tie-dye colored sunsets
But no one said a word
When they heard her
Ripped from earth's bed
She's so beautiful
Just had to have here physically dead
Chopped off her crown
Stupid frowns didn't form enough force
To stop the ax
No nerve to preserve Black women
Like we promote buying music on wax
Tracks in tune with sounds
Inside human beehives
Modusa's spirit stays alive
In after hour dives
On the east side
Where were you when she died?
And the death chant spread
That's a beautiful Black woman

So
Off with her head
Off with her head
That's what they said.

Where were you when she died?
And the death chant spread
That's a beautiful Black woman

So
Off with her head
Off with her head
That's what they said.

Keisha and other girls
who
dream with their eyes open

There is a mark in the path connecting reality with our souls
And I'll die there when I run out of poems
My home is where I slept last night divided by the number of breaths it takes me
to speak
Sometimes my pen has a slow leak writing weak-lipped excuses
That smack their teeth at me in the mirror

Don't you know Harlem hides holocaust survivors
Inside the sweet of Sugar Hill?
Live chocolate squares of little girls hop-scotch taped across mouths
Told to shut up

They talk with white chalk
Connecting invisible dots inside color-less books
That only look good when they are the studied subjects
But not the authors

You know my name is Keisha and the things I draw come true

My bones dig me up once a day
So I can watch the sun get hot at noon
Eat my morning chant while watching animated ghetto car tunes
Background music to drive-bys
So don't keep asking me why
I never stay inside the lines
My road is curved and not many have traveled the complexity of my

Simple

I hide time inside dimples

Smiling at the possibility of looking happy
Despite the cuts I got on my knuckles
From beating myself down just to keep my aspirations in check
Mama says I sound like a poet but she never reads my work
Instead she listens from the window
She threw me from

So I serenade the smell of time against my will
In the middle of a chocolate factory called Sugar Hill
I create pictures of what beautiful must look like
If I could draw it standing still

One Bad Brotha

With one gasp of brilliant breath
forming sentence
Lent his heart to
Millions
Of Christian saints searching
On Sunday
Found
Mecca on Monday
Never again to be the same
They came.
With smiles in friendly fire faces
Masked Media Manipulators
Interpreters
Of Untruths
Uncouth
Question asking
Basking
In our Black sky
Why
You wanna divide
Message from man
True separatist serpents
Spitting poison
On Black boys
And girls who
Recognize taste
Of table scraps
Slave Trap
Chills up my spine
Run and hide
Pork-bellied swine
Senate and House eating
Cheating on nation's children
Off beat
Without heart
Kill
Still
Millions of Drums

Made Magical Music on Monday
Mission Message
Catch this
Melanin Man Melody
Televised in a trance
VIP's at Elephants and Donkey
Dance
They came
Earth shaking
Hands
Without shackles
Wearing brown, yellow, tan and
Deep Black Brothas
Grandmothers Gold
Got aboard Bus
Without picnic basket
Goodies
Sporting Suit and Ties
Jeans and Hoodies
Could he
Be God?
Masculine Miracle
Creating Cradle
Of Civilization
Connecting energy
Over airwaves of
Black radio stations
King of Black nations
Concentration keeps
The Sky Clear
Fist of Fiery
Knuckles without fear
Locked lovely pieces
Of earth
Walked past in Tri-colored
Camouflage
Fighting our own war
Sitting in trees
Swimming in Black Man sea
You can't see

Our invisible souls
Revolutionary Troops
Shooting hoop
Came.
Gangsta Rapping
Savage Stealing
Dope Dealing
Crime Bill Killing
Us
Came.
Hat to the back
Church going brothas
Meat lovers and
Vegetarians
Came.
Three Hundred and
Sixty Degree
Driven
Giving dap
Faded hair, naturally napped
Came.
Teary eyed
Carrying baby boys on back
Sistas
Came.
Children hanging from daddy's
knees
Baggy jeans seemed to fall
Perfectly
They came
Traded Pounds and Plays
For Hugs
As we prayed

They came
Purse snatching
Without giving you
Expected Reaction
They Came
In peace
On October 16th
He called
Them to the mall
By just one name.
Millions of Black men
Won't ever be the same.

For Donald Goines to the third power

Dude
You never got to show us your dribble
I see you speaking Sybil
Searching for the saggy jeans approval
From big brotha lips
Same time got three years yelling
You're too young to know all that grown man shit
Black Girl Lost
Got pimp daddy veins shooting up   your gospel on Sunday
Singing the Peter Pan theme
Seemed like Washing your hair
as the crack cooked on iron
Stove was normal then
Not less than human then
Never had a chance to grab your gloc at   3 years old
You never knew how Motown
Sounded without the sound of gun shots sampled

Bleeding dreams of one day bicycle on two wheels
Peddling without Direction
Young hands follow Braile
Gangsta tales   We didn't know you understood
The bumps in the paper meant
You could die here
baby

Would you pass the 40 Over his head?
Your grand-daddy ain't gonna
ever die   Instead
We skip a generation   Go straight to genocide
Do Not Pass Go   Do not play with your tonka trucks
Do not ever grow up   Cause you a warrior baby
Do not leave us   Your work has just begun

How do we apologize for our drive-by attitudes?
Waiting for you to tell us with baby tears it's time to
Move on
That you will watch over adult infancy taking its first steps

Towards freedom
Ain't here cause we don't see uniformed war-torn soldiers
Dead in the middle of 7-mile Road
Ain't here cause there are miltary bases
under our sidewalks
Ready to blow away our play toys we call weapons
Ain't really here when G-I never knew the camougflage came
In Black
Young and lifted above Tickle-me Elmo dolls rainbow child

Wish you could help us now
Stop us from spitting up

Thirty Bottles of milk on the wall
Dirty Bottles of milk
Silk-wrapped we suspend our sorrow
In mid-air
Waiting for your spirit to capture our guilty wind
With your tiny wings
Will they write about your life as a street hustler
A genius among thieves   Who will grieve again
Before the books begin to repeat paragraphs   Never end
And your life is not your own
And your death is not your own
Cause you too damn young to create to own
Something so incredible so great so crazy
so graphic so sad

with your baby talk
with your baby walk

You could teach us how to speak more human
Treat our own people with grace
Guide us to a better place

Dude

Smile us into a friendlier world
Without friendly fire ripping apart your diaper
Snipers inside your gold dipped baby shoes

Stealing goo goos with grenades
Save us daddy cool genes for killing our prophets
For driving eldorado red
Into your playpen
No, you will never go out like that

NOT ALONE, DUDE

We will experience the new books you author
In our own blood baby
You will not sit among the Detroit library classics
Untitled
Donald Goines your daddy loves you, baby
To the third power

WHO WILL BE THE LAST POET?

This piece was originally written for Umar Bin Hassan and now I give it to the memory of Tupac Shakur, Notorious B.I.G. and poets around the world.

Who will be the last poet?
Paying dues to prove we know it all
I'm saying toward the East salaat/praying
We're gaining inner peace treaties
Smiling with silver spoons on boxes of wheaties
Eating bowls of sacrificed lambs
Cooking our craft like Sam
I was born by the river
When pure water deteriorate your liver
Giver of ghetto voice
Machete Mouth grenade
Everyone sips your spit adding flavor
To their piss-colored lemonade
Crazy ace of spade
Speaking in twisted scattered scorpio speak
Outsiders search for leaks
Hate to see you at your peak
Fake winks blown away with swift brushes of ink
Compete for props
Blow up the spot
Freedom fighter
Revolution inspired
Liars wisdom on wasted energy
Trying to see me
Boomeranging unfounded breaths of negativity
What you hate about me
You hate more about yourself
Wealth cannot buy self love
Bloody gloves Fit finger pointers
Anointers of analytical arguments
Flared
They were the first to tell us
Niggas are scared
E Equals M-C squared
So why do your lyrics lack
Well- rounded energy?

Root of spoken trees blown away
As we smoke weed
Drinking herbal tea
Defining me
With plastic score cards
Compromising without realizing
This used to be a movement
Political platform
Means writing poetic porn
Getting some revolutionary ass
On the college dorm floor
Deep in the heart of Harlem
Spirits and sporadic microphone sex
Test the status quo
How many poets gotta go?
Who will make it out
Before we choke on clout
Greed and sweaty palm
Pimps and prostitutes
Make the best poets
Hustlers and hijackers
Convicted felons
Thieves stealing watermelon seeds
From kids at picnics deserve
Pulitzer prizes
Literary recognition
For being literally what they claim to be
Cutting down cherry trees
Unafraid don't flee
Poets sitting on Santa's knee
Wishing for a war we could win
With a ball-point pen
Ink blots block out the true meaning of life
Poets packing guns and bladed knife
Kill the voice
Chock-holding heroes
You get a zero
For owning mental locks without roots
Tongues that shoot blanks
Yanked from the ranks

UN honorable dis-charge
Without purple heart
You the man today
Gonna blow up this cafe' anyway
M-80 toting lady
Drowning your selfishness
Beneath the Euphrates
I'd rather trade these young hands
Gripping glass
Black girl juice dripping down your throat
So you can taste what you could've had
Sad Spiritual schizo
What a poet know?
How low can we really go?
When the ego self destructs
Like plastic legos
Who'll build evil empires
Poet for hire
You're fired
For not continuing the legacy
One of the first quenching hoodlum thirst
Hoodlum thirst
Holding educators and politicians -- At pen point
As we steal truth
Tracking our arms with addictive scars
Cause our people have been fiending for centuries
Your voice always so clear to me
Please stop all this madness
Please stop all this madness
For our poetic fathers
All seven
It's the 11th Hour
Poetic showers don't always get off
Mud shoved between crippled African toes
There goes
One more, two or three
Nothing worse than a slave free
Killing his own family
Forcing tubes down throat
Can't forget what you wrote

Don't you ever float...float on!
Till the break of dawn
Poets are being born
As we speak about the art form
Pregnant with metaphors, music, moonlight
And microphones

You are our open door
After a long walk home
Your stones skip rocks and wave to wannabees
Trees bow their knees
Wooden broomsticks wither and cry
Cause they lost the chance
To sweep you off your feet
Repeat!
Who will be the last poet?
Show it off
Your sexy big red "S" Poetically undressed your lyrics are skinny
Carved like thanksgiving turkey
Your breasts are juicy
But the milk is stolen
Swinging swollen fists
Miss every time
My words are wind
Blowing past you
Can't kill original rhyme creators
You brought rhythm and revolution
Extinct like eagle
Soaring into the souls of black folk
Live what you wrote
Write while you're still alive
How many will die?
For the last chance
Complacent with southern comfort
With no proof or poetic license
Rolling dice and shooting craps
Against concrete curbs
That elevate us above the earth
Still remaining grounded
There are shoes to fill

On the long walk home
So we adjust our tongues
Tie our young laces
Races end up at the starting line
Time is not finished
So throw your hands in the air
Above your heads
For old times sake
Take your manhood and lie it face down
On the cold cement
Check it in Black poet
You are well read books

Hard undercovers
Language lovers
Turning truthful page
Raging rivers rescue real revolutionaries
Cause even water gets thirsty
Returning to the well
Throwing pennies into black holes
Wishing words were worthy of our expression
We have leaned since the first day you decided
To show it
Not everyone will make it out alive
Who will be the last poet?

Read this— if it applies to you!

I don't know the first names of
all my true supporters
but I know they've never doubted my work

Strangers prayed for me to win
Not because it would help the poetry scene
blow up
But because I was talking to them

I never heard the ones who didn't think
My poetry was all that great
Ever say it to me
directly
But I can recall that young sista in the
Village with long beautiful scars on her face
Telling me she was a poet too

And those brothas with leather coats and
hustler gangsta lean Martel holding hands
Giving me pounds without pretentious smiles
At Legends nightclub in Detroit
No, I didn't know the science behind how the applause meter worked Didn't
do the research
I just read my poem for Harlem
The way I always read it for my girls
For Trea, for Charlotte, for Lynn
I didn't buy a new outfit or get my hair done
I'm sorry if your concentration on how "cute I am" interrupts your ability to
pay attention
but why underestimate the rest of us?
I never needed a trendy kiss on the cheek validation from poets still wet inked
behind their ears
Cause I can remember the faces and the rush of all those children Playing in
Morningside park uptown who wanted my name on pieces of dirty brown
paper bag
And the little pigtailed girl who left her swing screaming to her friends
"That's the poet from the Apollo!"
And that's validation enough

There are many other places where everyday folks live
Who create art without the artistic community as a comfortable backdrop
Like the Underground Railroad in Richmond, my people in Nashville, Patrick
at the Kuumba Kafe in Little Rock, the sistas working at the South Carolina
movie theater inside the mall who wanted to hear "Black Girl Juice," in front
of the popcorn machine, to the women who gave me love at the passport
office, and to all the young men on the street who said, "Yo, I love your work.
Good Luck, baby" And to
visual artists like Wendell Brown who gave me, a stranger, a piece of his own
beautiful inspiration because he simply believed me
Trusted my spirit through a televised looking glass
Or the young brotha Imhotep Newsome at New Rochelle High School
Who wrote two poems for me on the spot

Have you ever been there?
Away from the safety of home
Where I am
Now in Brooklyn among the Mecca of
beautiful voices

I am not trying to represent
A borough or any country for that matter

I am a poet
black female and 25
Like Nikki was
I am not the second coming of a woman
who's still writing poetry in Virginia

I am a Moore like my daddy

Drinking English Tea like my mum
Attempting to live and love what I do
And poetry is only a part of that

These poems are for all my people
who give me love just because
in some way without knowing
I gave it unselfishly to them
And it's the highest compliment I've ever been given
And I hope to somehow thank you with this poem
So please read this
If it applies to you

Is It revolutionary for a woman to cook her man dinner?

Is it revolutionary for a woman to cook her man dinner?
If you make love before marriage are you really a sinner?
Wearing red, black and green means you're trying to move
back to Africa
You have long, stringy blond hair, so you listen to Metallica.
Rock and Roll, Hip Hop Jazz or Soul
Melting Pot or Salad Bowl
Gold on your neck
or covering your front teeth

I stay away from pork, so I'm a muslim who eats no meat
I went to church on Sunday, so now I'm sanctified
My eyes start tearing when I'm chopping onion, but over you
I never cried.
Tried to keep my composure when I told you that last lie
People are always saying hello when they want to say goodbye
You're a Pan-Africanist by day, and at night
bake American Apple Pies
Is it revolutionary to grow dreads, then never get a job?
Your friends call you black, your co-workers call you bob.
Doesn't it seem like the guilty folks always point the finger?
Wait. Is it revolutionary for a woman to cook her man dinner?

I need to know, cause folks are caught up on fake perceptions
they must make up in their sleep.
Just because you burn incense doesn't mean that you're deep
I heard your mama pays the notes on your red cherokee-indian jeep
You take trips on planes, ride in big automobiles
So why is the government still paying your bills?
The thrill is gone
I hate Fila flip-flop tongs
Skinny women always wishing for hips, and thick woman make themselves
sick to get thinner
So, is it revolutionary to want to make your man dinner?
Independently I am man-WO, Wo-man.
Long tailored skirt for work
Or cooking with a frying pan

I bring home the turkey bacon

But, wanting to chill with my man
is something I'm not fakin'!
Taking control and being on your own is all good and fair.
But, when I get home from work I want him to wash my hair
Breast implants explode before their time
See, I can make the wind sing, without hanging out a chime.
Man-Wo, Wo-man.
I'm done shopping for bargains at Sears
I've got a brand new credit card, and I'm charging away all my fears
Don't ever gamble, so I'm always a winner
So, is it revolutionary to want to set out the plates, light two candles and watch your man slowly eat your dinner.
Tying that white apron around a tired nine to five body
Putting the kids bed, and wiping three noses that were snotty
I've got this delicious new recipe
In the kitchen can't nobody mess with me
I'm okay where I'm at right now, so I guess that means I've made it to heaven
Yea, I just got off at five, but baby, dinner will be ready at Seven.
Isn't that scary?
I guess being a housewife warrior working woman
Can really be

Revolutionary

The sweetest revolutionary

My evening gown is guerrilla green
I make offerings of myself before the first of every month
Cause there are bills to be paid
Instead of getting laid I prostitute verbs manipulate whispers
Defined as words
Saying shit we've already heard
But not quite like that

See, I know she-poets who'll
squeeze nippled hard headed trees
At their knees
Just so their men will name them honey
Haikued hips dripping 17 syllables of sweat
Drying you off with sunset breath
Still he ain't feeling you yet?

Tongue-tied you travel on top of yellow bees
Hiding your real sting cause he likes the quiet type
cool yeah right-right right-right
You search your belly adjust your skully
Hoping to find some sexy sentence hiding between revolution
and rhyme making

Damn he's throwing my poem off
Got the nerve to sit in the front row/on my front porch/on my living room
faux Asian throw rug/In my bathroom/on my mahogany paisley throw/
down on my bedroom futon.
I'm trippin'

But he blends so well with the pillows
there are reasons I'm not supposed to look at brothas like you
Telling me I betta write harder/talk louder/sing protest lyrics/keep my
stomach flat/where my hair in a politically correct style/smile and wink
between oppression/Then out-do the male poets/was his confession

Like I'm wearing left over pink frilly prom dress lace under my brown kufi
got a six pack of gunfire in my garter
I'm a bowl of mashed potatoes from scratch cooking martyr

Yeah a war torn Detroit born bush baby when you unbutton my belly telescope tenderoni
A turkey bologna with two knife slits fried in butter bitch
One of them deep hoes
Those abstract poetic tricks you wanna get with
When the cafe' rhetoric smoke clears
Got true fears of feline lick cleaned culture kitty cats that you meow at
When the jeans look tight as we weigh in on invisible scales on stage
How many pounds of black rage can your love - handle?

Still miracle our way wearing brown sandals carrying seeds on our sultry saddles flipping the pancake spattle shaking the snakes off baby rattles
Got to be head wrapped when we haiku/You love the way I seduce with my blues even If I cry when I sing

Cause baby we can do ANYTHING excuse has abused us into believing
We cannot fine china break cause we eat earthquakes during snack breaks
Double dutch during dramas of who-dun-it when I know the most wanted by first names
meditation on solar plexus erects us into blue candle light perfection A hot bath water affection nourishes our naked nature numbed by unnatural nine to fives that need more than calgon to make the ugly of the world wash away
Make our black butterfly spirits feel simply
make it through the day   -   okay

wings wobble and weaken as the star-spangled banner swings billy clubbed choruses and horses the voices of our children's throats forced to sing slave to grave dreams that die when fire works don't burn our names in branded flames
And you steady throwing me what's up baby game at my frame?
Admit to trying to get my flirt on while I file my nails down for the frontlines or the free throw

Whichever comes first

There is a thirst in wanting to let you drink my hot cocoa mango lips
That can't convince you that my work is never done
And my night oil races a sun showing up on my doorstep with long-stemmed doubt

-For the sweetest revolutionary-

When the vase lacks spiritual base   politically imprisoned
passion petals can't grow broken hearted
It seems so romantic and cute to get started
But I need to finish my next book
Containing complete thoughts not part time wants
Knowing Marvin Gaye died the night before his birth
Is why I hurry and you worry that my life work may kill me
Before you ever get a chance to kiss my face
When I really just need my voice hugged
My spirit loved
And a little time to work being a woman
Into my busy schedule
America offers advil in place of menstrual huts
So we press our ear lobes against our ovaries listening
For our childrens footsteps cramping our style as we
Keel over on concrete tile painting on smiles so
No one will know we really want to fly south for the winter
With the rest of the black eyed birds
Leaving white stained relief on curious teeth
Looking up our winged skirts
You blew your purple silk breath of fresh air into my fertile sand-colored belly
And now the dust got in your eyes so you can no longer find the sexy in me
between my knees
Talking about "Get your poem on baby"
 "You a fine revolutionary lady!"
Wanna Wade me in the water but not help me raise our
 daughter?
Imbalanced we dance with americanized feet that never remove shoes and
don't know how to walk one block with laundry baskets on our heads

Instead we wed dollar signs fornicate for dimes corporate climb
Trying to get work on time blowing kisses at positive rhymes
That can't get you a deal
So it's hard for us to deal

For REAL

I'm the MC's wife in search of an angel to untangle vocal cords wrapped
around my neck plugged into misogynous microphones making me bob my
membrane to my own gang bang

You think I don't matter
So my voice turns to matter
Squeezed so small It no longer occupies space
Yet It's still here
Hiding in the center of black holes in my panty hoes
So loud clear nail polish can't cover it up
I'm pregnant with potential but I birth silence
And just cause you slap me on my ass doesn't mean I'll scream
For you
My private is braided into pigtails decorated plastic barrettes and yellow rubber bands
The little girl in me is afraid
But the woman in me will kill you
While cooking breakfast
That's that Scorpio shit
You get caught up on wanting to menage' trois my metaphor five six times a
lady third eye invade me
We drown in lyrical libations never played on radio stations
Hands grow impatient

and I want to be sweet for you baby
but your spit no longer drips liquid sugar
teeth are rotting and falling as I speak
to my spirit alone with my things to do list
standing on my spine before realizing your feet are too heavy
for my back so I simply erase your name
from the paper
wet the dead tree with my tears in hopes to grow a dozen more
of you so afraid
To let me show you how a real woman could
help you find the man in you
My wholeness will guide you to the half of you
you thought you didn't have
so you only offered the little that your body allowed
And in the end it's never enough
cause
I wanna smell like it
taste like it feel like it walk barefoot inside it
wrap it around my waist wear it in the shower take it home with me
share it with my girls play an Aretha C-D to it

128

eat it sweat it believe it African dance to it wash my face with it hold it love it grow it out my stomach rock my adidas with it let it run down my back lick it live it shake a tambourine and say an amen because of it steal it if I have to melt chocolate on top of it

just want it to be sweet baby
sweet like you like we can be
like revolution